AI AGENTS IN PRACTICE

Concepts, Code, and Deployment

By

Dr. Hesham Mohamed Elsherif

About the Author

Dr. Hesham Mohamed Elsherif stands at the forefront of library management and research, boasting an impressive 22-year tenure in the field. Holding dual doctoral degrees, one in Management and Organizational Leadership and the other in Information Systems and Technology, Dr. Elsherif brings a unique blend of knowledge to any intellectual endeavor.

An expert in Empirical research methodology, Dr. Elsherif specializes particularly in the Qualitative approach and Action research. This specialization has not only strengthened his research endeavors but has also allowed him to contribute invaluable insights and advancements in these areas.

Over the years, Dr. Elsherif has made significant contributions to the academic world not only as a professional researcher but also as an Adjunct Professor. This multifaceted role in the educational landscape has further solidified his reputation as a thought leader and pioneer.

Furthermore, Dr. Elsherif's expertise isn't confined to one region. He has served as a consultant to numerous educational institutions on an international scale, sharing best practices, innovative strategies, and his deep insights into the ever-evolving realms of management and technology.

Combining a passion for education with an unparalleled depth of knowledge, Dr. Elsherif continues to inspire, educate, and lead in both the library and academic communities.

Preface

Artificial Intelligence (AI) is no longer a concept bound to the pages of science fiction or limited to research laboratories. Today, AI permeates our daily lives—from smart assistants guiding us through our day, autonomous vehicles navigating complex environments, to advanced systems managing critical operations in industries like healthcare, finance, and logistics. At the heart of these intelligent systems are AI agents, entities designed to perceive their environment, make decisions, and act autonomously to achieve specific goals.

Yet, despite the proliferation and evident benefits of AI agents, there's often a substantial gap between theoretical concepts and practical implementation. This gap leaves many students, developers, and even experienced practitioners struggling to translate theoretical knowledge into functional, deployable solutions.

"AI Agents in Practice: Concepts, Code, and Deployment" is specifically crafted to bridge this divide. It offers a clear, step-by-step journey that begins with fundamental concepts, progresses through detailed hands-on implementation, and culminates in professional-level deployment strategies. Our goal is not just to inform but to empower you to build, deploy, and manage AI agents confidently, regardless of whether you're a beginner, an intermediate developer, or a seasoned professional looking to sharpen your skills.

Throughout this book, you will:

- Grasp foundational concepts and architectures underpinning various types of AI agents.

- Develop practical coding skills by implementing agents from simple reflexive types to sophisticated deep reinforcement learning systems.
- Understand deployment strategies crucial for transforming experimental agents into robust, scalable real-world applications.
- Explore crucial ethical, security, and governance considerations to ensure responsible AI practices.
- Benefit from in-depth, real-world case studies that highlight successes, challenges, and practical insights.

To ensure accessibility, this book assumes only basic familiarity with programming and a general understanding of algorithms. It methodically builds your skills and confidence, combining clarity in explanation with hands-on coding exercises, practical deployment examples, and professional best practices.

Whether your aim is to deepen your professional expertise, to pioneer innovations, or simply to better understand the rapidly evolving world of AI, this book serves as your practical guide, equipping you with the knowledge and tools needed to thrive in a future increasingly defined by intelligent systems.

Let's dive in and demystify AI agents, transforming theory into tangible, impactful practice.

Dr. Hesham Mohamed Elsherif

Who Should Read This Book?

This book is designed for a diverse group of readers who share a common interest in understanding, building, and deploying AI agents - whether you're completely new to artificial intelligence, an experienced developer looking to dive deeper into AI-driven systems, or a professional aiming to enhance your skills for real-world implementation. Specifically, this book is beneficial for:

Students and Academics:
If you're studying computer science, data science, or engineering and want to bridge theoretical knowledge with practical skills, this book will provide both foundational concepts and hands-on projects. You'll learn how AI agents function, explore relevant algorithms, and practice building your own agents from scratch.

Software Developers and Engineers:
Developers familiar with programming but new to artificial intelligence will find clear explanations and practical code examples to smoothly transition into building intelligent agents. This book assumes familiarity with basic programming concepts, making it easier for you to dive directly into implementation and professional-grade deployment.

Data Scientists and Analysts:
Professionals in data science seeking to expand their toolkit with AI agent-based solutions will appreciate sections on advanced machine learning techniques, particularly deep reinforcement learning, multi-agent environments, and practical NLP integrations. The material presented will help you translate complex AI theories into actionable insights and functioning systems.

Technical Managers and IT Professionals:
If you're managing or overseeing projects involving AI technology, understanding AI agents deeply can significantly enhance decision-

making, project planning, and implementation strategies. You'll gain insights into how these technologies can practically benefit your organization, including best practices for deploying robust and scalable AI systems.

Entrepreneurs and Innovators:
Individuals looking for innovation opportunities through AI-powered solutions will find valuable guidance on applying AI agent concepts in diverse real-world scenarios—from startups to large-scale industry applications. The case studies and deployment sections will help you identify practical pathways and realistic challenges in launching successful AI-driven products.

In short, if you're curious about how intelligent software can make autonomous decisions, act on your behalf, or automate complex tasks, this book offers a comprehensive resource from foundational concepts all the way through professional-grade development and deployment.

Table of Contents

Part 1: Foundations of AI Agents 14

Chapter 1: Understanding AI Agents 14

What is an AI Agent? 14

Types of AI Agents 18

Examples of AI Agents in Real-World Applications 22

Chapter 2: Core Concepts and Theory 25

Intelligent Agent Architectures 25

Agent Environments 28

Perception, Reasoning, Action, and Learning in AI Agents 32

Rationality and Optimality in Decision-Making 36

Chapter 3: Essential AI Technologies and Algorithms 41

Search Algorithms 41

Decision-Making Under Uncertainty 45

Reinforcement Learning (Q-Learning, Deep RL) 49

Planning and Scheduling Algorithms 53

Part 2: Building AI Agents from Scratch 59

Chapter 4: Setting Up Your Environment 59

Languages: Python, R, and JavaScript 59

Essential Libraries and Frameworks 63

Chapter 5: Basic Agent Implementation 68

Creating a Simple Reflex Agent 68

Building Rule-Based Agents 72

Hands-on Example: Simple Game-Playing Agent 76

Chapter 6: Advanced Agent Architectures 80

Implementing Model-Based and Goal-Driven Agents 80

Creating a Utility-Based Decision-Making System 84
Hands-on Example: Basic Agent Navigation System 89
Part 3: Professional Development and Advanced Techniques 95
Chapter 7: Machine Learning for AI Agents 95
Supervised, Unsupervised, and Reinforcement Learning 95
Deep Reinforcement Learning 99
Implementing Learning-Based Agents from Scratch 103
Chapter 8: Multi-Agent Systems 108
Fundamentals of Multi-Agent Environments 108
Coordination, Collaboration, and Competition Strategies 111
Real-World Examples (Autonomous Vehicles, Robotics) 115
Chapter 9: Natural Language Processing in AI Agents 119
Chatbots and Conversational Agents 119
Implementing NLP in Agent Interactions 124
Case Studies 128
Part 4: Deployment and Practical Applications 132
Chapter 10: Deployment Strategies for AI Agents 132
Containerization and Docker 132
Cloud Deployment 136
Edge Deployment Considerations 140
Best Practices for Scalable Systems 145
Chapter 11: Security, Ethics, and Governance 149
Ethical Considerations in AI Agent Deployment 149
Security Challenges and Solutions 152
Compliance and Governance in AI Systems 156
Chapter 12: Real-World Case Studies 160
Industry-Specific AI Agent Deployments 160

Lessons Learned and Practical Insights 162
Insights from Industry Experts 166
Part 5: Looking Forward 170
Chapter 13: Emerging Trends and Future Directions 170
Trends in Autonomous Decision-Making Agents 170
Explainable and Transparent AI Agents 174
Human-Agent Collaboration Scenarios 177
Future Challenges and Research Directions 180
Appendices 185
Appendix A: Mathematical Foundations 185
Appendix B: Useful Resources 188
Appendix C: Glossary of Terms and Acronyms 192

Overview of AI Agents

Artificial Intelligence agents, or AI agents, are entities designed to interact intelligently with their environments to perform specific tasks autonomously. At their core, AI agents perceive their surroundings, reason or make decisions based on their perceptions, and then act accordingly to achieve predetermined goals. This fundamental capability makes AI agents suitable for a vast array of applications, ranging from simple automation tasks to complex strategic planning.

Defining AI Agents

An AI agent is defined by its ability to perceive its environment through sensors and act upon that environment through actuators. In practical terms, sensors might include cameras, microphones, or data inputs, while actuators could involve robotic arms, motors, speech systems, or digital interfaces. The primary goal of an AI agent is to continuously perform the perceive-decide-act cycle to reach a defined objective.

Types of AI Agents

AI agents can be categorized into several distinct types, each characterized by their complexity and behavior:

1. **Simple Reflex Agents:**
    - Operate based solely on current perceptions.
    - Use condition-action rules that directly map perceived states to actions.
    - Example: Thermostat controlling room temperature.

2. **Model-Based Agents:**
    - Maintain an internal state or model of the world.
    - Utilize perceptions and internal states to make decisions.
    - Example: Autonomous vehicles that predict future states based on past observations.
3. **Goal-Based Agents:**
    - Incorporate explicit goals or desired outcomes in decision-making.
    - Choose actions by considering their consequences relative to their goals.
    - Example: Navigation systems selecting routes based on destination.
4. **Utility-Based Agents:**
    - Evaluate actions based on a utility function, optimizing satisfaction or performance metrics.
    - Make decisions by maximizing expected utility.
    - Example: Trading bots optimizing financial returns.
5. **Learning Agents:**
    - Continuously improve their performance based on experiences.
    - Employ methods such as reinforcement learning, supervised learning, or unsupervised learning.
    - Example: Game-playing AI improving through repeated play.

Agent Environments

AI agents operate in various environments, which significantly influence their design and functioning. Key distinctions among agent environments include:

- **Fully Observable vs. Partially Observable:** Availability of complete information at all times versus limited or uncertain information.
- **Deterministic vs. Stochastic:** Predictable outcomes versus randomness and uncertainty.
- **Static vs. Dynamic:** Stable and unchanged environments versus continuously evolving situations.
- **Discrete vs. Continuous:** Clearly defined states and actions versus infinite possibilities.

Real-World Applications

AI agents are extensively deployed across multiple industries, demonstrating their versatility:

- **Robotics:** Autonomous robots for manufacturing, exploration, or healthcare.
- **Automotive:** Self-driving vehicles using complex sensing and decision-making processes.
- **Finance:** Automated trading and portfolio management systems optimizing financial transactions.
- **Healthcare:** Intelligent diagnostic tools and patient monitoring systems.
- **Customer Service:** Chatbots and virtual assistants enhancing customer interactions and support.

Understanding these fundamentals and recognizing their practical implications will set the stage for deeper exploration into building, deploying, and scaling AI agents effectively throughout this book.

Part 1: Foundations of AI Agents
Chapter 1: Understanding AI Agents

What is an AI Agent?

At the heart of Artificial Intelligence lies the concept of the AI agent. Simply put, an AI agent is a system that perceives its environment, reasons about what to do, and takes actions to achieve specific goals. The agent is designed to act autonomously, processing inputs from its environment and responding appropriately based on a decision-making framework, often derived from rules, models, or learned behaviors.

The definition of an AI agent can be formalized as:

- An AI agent is anything that can perceive its environment through sensors and act upon that environment through actuators, based on some decision-making process.

This basic interaction of perception, reasoning, and action is the foundation for all AI agents, whether they're embedded in robotics, chatbots, autonomous vehicles, or game-playing agents.

The Sense-Think-Act Cycle

An AI agent operates on a loop of three main stages:

1. **Perception**: The agent senses the environment, which could include visual data, sensory inputs (like touch or sound), or even abstract information such as market trends or user commands. The agent processes this information into a usable form called *percepts*.
2. **Reasoning or Decision Making**: The agent uses algorithms, learned models, or pre-defined rules to make decisions based on

its perceptions. The decision could involve selecting an action from a set of possible actions that best serves its goals.

3. **Action**: Based on its decision, the agent acts within its environment. This action could be moving a robot arm, responding to a user query, or adjusting a recommendation system's output.

The process continually repeats itself, allowing the agent to adjust its behavior based on changes in the environment or new information. This is illustrated below:

The AI Agent Cycle: A Visual Explanation

```
+----------------+
|  Perception  |   <-- (Sensory Input: Environment)
+----------------+
       |
       v
+----------------+
| Decision/Reasoning|   <-- (Algorithms, Models, or Rules)
+----------------+
       |
       v
+----------------+
|   Action     |   <-- (Agent's Response to Environment)
+----------------+
       |
       v
+----------------+
|  Environment  |   <-- (State Change due to Action)
+----------------+
```

Key Components of an AI Agent

1. Sensors (Perception Module):

The *sensors* are responsible for gathering information about the environment. These sensors can be hardware (like cameras, microphones, or temperature sensors in robotics) or software-based (like web scraping, database queries, or reading input data). The *perception module* converts this raw data into percepts that the agent can understand and act upon.

2. Decision-Making / Reasoning:

This is the core of the agent, where the actual intelligence happens. Depending on the complexity of the agent, this can involve simple decision trees, machine learning models, or sophisticated planning algorithms. The agent must use its current state and goals to determine the most appropriate action to take.

For example, in a **game-playing agent**, the reasoning might involve choosing the best move based on a minimax tree or a reinforcement learning model.

3. Actuators (Action Module):

The *actuators* are responsible for executing the agent's decisions. In a robot, this could involve moving motors or moving limbs, while in a digital assistant, this could be generating a response or triggering an API call. The agent's actions cause changes in the environment, which are then perceived again in the next cycle.

AI Agent Types: Simple to Complex

AI agents vary widely in their sophistication. They can be categorized into different types based on their complexity:

1. **Simple Reflex Agents**:
   These agents act based on the current percept, usually through condition-action rules. For example, if a robot detects an obstacle, it may immediately reverse direction. Simple reflex agents can handle basic, predefined scenarios but lack memory or adaptability.
2. **Model-Based Reflex Agents**:
   These agents maintain an internal model of the world and use this model to make decisions. Unlike simple reflex agents, they are capable of handling partially observable environments by

storing information about the past. For example, a vacuum-cleaning robot might remember where it has already cleaned to avoid redundant actions.

3. **Goal-Based Agents**:
   These agents can plan and act to achieve specific goals. They can reason about different courses of action to reach their objective, considering multiple steps and contingencies. For instance, a self-driving car's goal could be to reach a destination safely, navigating obstacles and adjusting its route in real-time.
4. **Utility-Based Agents**:
   These agents not only pursue goals but also evaluate various actions in terms of a *utility function*, choosing the action that maximizes some measure of "happiness" or "usefulness." These agents are useful in complex environments where multiple goals must be balanced. For example, in a business setting, an agent may aim to optimize both profits and customer satisfaction.
5. **Learning Agents**:
   These are the most advanced agents, capable of improving their performance through experience. Learning agents use techniques like **reinforcement learning** to adapt and learn from interactions with the environment. Over time, they modify their behavior to maximize long-term success, such as improving the performance of a stock trading algorithm or a game-playing AI like AlphaGo.

Real-World Examples of AI Agents

- **Autonomous Vehicles**: Self-driving cars use a variety of sensors (cameras, LiDAR, radar) to perceive the environment, plan their route, and control the vehicle to reach a destination safely. The agent must handle real-time data from dynamic environments and continuously learn from past experiences.
- **Robotic Assistants**: Robots in warehouses or homes, like those used by Amazon or robotic vacuums (e.g., Roomba), make decisions based on their environment. They sense obstacles, plan

their movements, and take actions like navigating a space or picking up objects.

- **Virtual Assistants**: AI agents like Siri, Alexa, or Google Assistant listen to user commands, reason about what the user wants, and perform actions, such as sending a message, controlling smart devices, or fetching information.
- **Recommendation Systems**: Platforms like Netflix, Spotify, or Amazon use AI agents to recommend products or content to users based on their preferences. These systems perceive user behavior, reason about possible preferences, and take actions to suggest the most relevant options.

In summary, An AI agent is a powerful computational entity that perceives, reasons, and acts within its environment. It forms the foundation of intelligent systems by automating decision-making, responding to dynamic changes in its surroundings, and often learning to improve its actions over time. From simple rule-based systems to advanced self-learning agents, AI agents are at the core of numerous modern technologies, ranging from robotics to virtual assistants, and play a critical role in how artificial intelligence is applied in real-world systems. Understanding the architecture, types, and capabilities of AI agents is essential to mastering the field of AI and its applications.

Types of AI Agents

Artificial Intelligence agents differ widely in their complexity, capabilities, and decision-making strategies. To grasp the foundational understanding necessary to build and deploy effective agents, it's crucial to explore the different types clearly and systematically. The five primary categories of AI agents, from simplest to most sophisticated, include:

1. Simple Reflex Agents

Definition:

Simple reflex agents act based solely on the current percept. They follow a straightforward, condition-action rule system. If a certain condition is met, a predefined action follows immediately.

Example:

A thermostat turning on a heater when room temperature drops below a certain threshold.

Advantages and Limitations:

- *Advantages*: Easy to design and implement, fast response.
- *Limitations*: Unable to handle complex situations, no memory of past states or events.

2. Model-Based Reflex Agents

Definition:

These agents extend simple reflex agents by incorporating an internal state that helps them handle partially observable environments. The internal model stores information about past percepts and actions to infer and maintain a notion of the world.

Example:

A robotic vacuum cleaner that remembers previously visited locations to avoid redundant cleaning.

Advantages and Limitations:

- *Advantages*: Better equipped to deal with partial visibility or uncertainty.
- *Limitations*: Still lacks proactive planning or goal-directed behavior.

3. Goal-Based Agents

Definition:

Goal-based agents select their actions according to explicitly defined goals. Unlike reflex agents, they can consider multiple steps ahead and plan strategically to reach their objectives, typically using search and planning algorithms.

Example:

Navigation systems in autonomous vehicles planning routes to reach a destination while handling dynamic road conditions.

Advantages and Limitations:

- *Advantages*: Able to plan, manage complex tasks, and adapt to changes in pursuit of clearly defined goals.
- *Limitations*: Goal clarity required; doesn't handle conflicts between competing goals without additional mechanisms.

4. Utility-Based Agents

Definition:

Utility-based agents enhance goal-based agents by quantifying outcomes with a utility function, helping the agent choose among multiple goals or uncertain outcomes. Utility functions enable agents to measure trade-offs, deciding not only how to reach a goal but how to optimize overall satisfaction.

Example:

An AI-powered investment manager choosing portfolios to maximize financial returns while balancing risk.

Advantages and Limitations:

- *Advantages*: Handles complex decision-making scenarios where multiple criteria must be balanced.
- *Limitations*: Requires precise formulation of the utility function, which can be challenging.

5. Learning Agents

Definition:

Learning agents improve their performance through feedback, typically by adapting their actions based on past experiences. They employ algorithms like reinforcement learning to refine decision-making strategies dynamically over time.

Example:

AI agents in gaming environments (like AlphaGo) learning through continuous gameplay to improve strategies.

Advantages and Limitations:

- *Advantages*: Adaptable and continuously improving; excellent for dynamic and unpredictable environments.
- *Limitations*: Complexity of implementation; requires significant training data or extensive interaction.

Understanding the Progression of AI Agent Complexity

The visual diagram above illustrates the progression from simple, reactive agents toward more advanced, proactive, and adaptive agents. Starting with simple reflex agents and moving toward learning agents, complexity increases through:

- Adding internal models (memory)
- Incorporating explicit goal-driven planning
- Evaluating actions based on utility or desirability
- Adapting and improving performance through continuous learning

This conceptual framework helps developers and researchers determine which agent type best matches their project's needs and context, ultimately allowing more targeted, effective AI system development.

Types of AI Agents: From Simple to Advanced

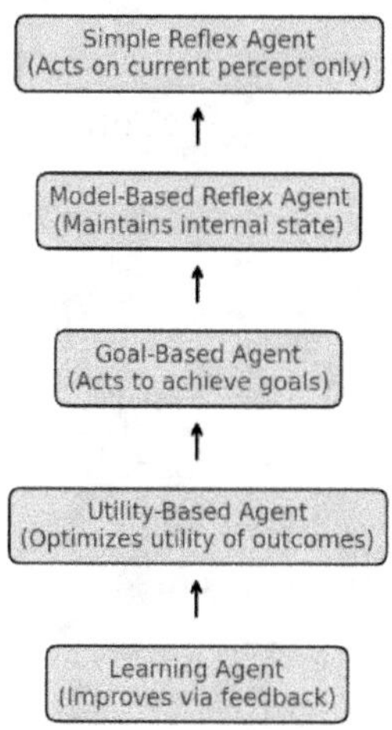

Examples of AI Agents in Real-World Applications

AI agents have become pervasive across industries. They all share the fundamental sense–think–act cycle but differ in sensors, decision logic, actuators, and learning capacity, tailored to specific domains:

Autonomous Vehicles

- **Perception**: Cameras, LiDAR, radar, GPS for mapping, obstacle detection, and localization.
- **Decision**: Path planning (e.g., A*, Dijkstra), sensor fusion, behavior prediction of other road users.
- **Action**: Steering, acceleration, braking.
- **Agent Type**: Model-based reflex agents enhanced with goal-based planning and reinforcement learning for lane changes, obstacle avoidance, and optimized routing.

Virtual Assistants

- **Perception**: Speech-to-text conversion, natural language understanding (NLU) via transformers or intent classifiers.
- **Decision**: Dialogue management systems or neural conversational models determine user intent and select appropriate responses or API calls.
- **Action**: Text-to-speech synthesis, API invocation (setting alarms, querying information).
- **Agent Type**: Goal-based agents augmented with utility functions to rank possible responses and continuous learning to improve dialogue fluency.

Recommendation Systems

- **Perception**: User interaction logs, ratings, purchase history.
- **Decision**: Collaborative filtering, matrix factorization, or deep embedding models to infer user preferences.
- **Action**: Present personalized item or content recommendations.
- **Agent Type**: Utility-based agents that optimize for metrics like click-through rate or user retention, often with bandit algorithms or reinforcement learning for exploration–exploitation balance.

Industrial Automation

- **Perception**: Machine-vision cameras, force/torque sensors, conveyor-belt flow sensors.
- **Decision**: Rule-based logic, state machines for standard operations, plus anomaly detection with unsupervised learning to flag maintenance needs.
- **Action**: Control robotic arms, sort packages, adjust conveyor speeds.
- **Agent Type**: Model-based reflex agents for routine tasks, goal-based agents for multi-step assembly processes, and learning agents for predictive maintenance.

Trading Systems

- **Perception**: Real-time market data feeds, order book changes, economic news sentiment.
- **Decision**: Algorithmic strategies (statistical arbitrage, mean reversion) or reinforcement learning agents optimizing reward functions linked to profit and risk.
- **Action**: Automated buy/sell orders, portfolio rebalancing at high frequency.
- **Agent Type**: Utility-based agents for risk–return optimization, evolving into learning agents that adapt strategies to market regime changes.

Healthcare Diagnostics

- **Perception**: Medical imaging (X-rays, MRI), patient vitals, electronic health records.
- **Decision**: Deep learning models (CNNs, transformer architectures) identify anomalies or predict disease risk; decision-support algorithms suggest treatment paths.
- **Action**: Generate diagnostic reports, alert clinicians to critical conditions, schedule follow-up procedures.
- **Agent Type**: Learning agents that improve accuracy through continual training on new patient data, with utility functions balancing diagnostic sensitivity and specificity.

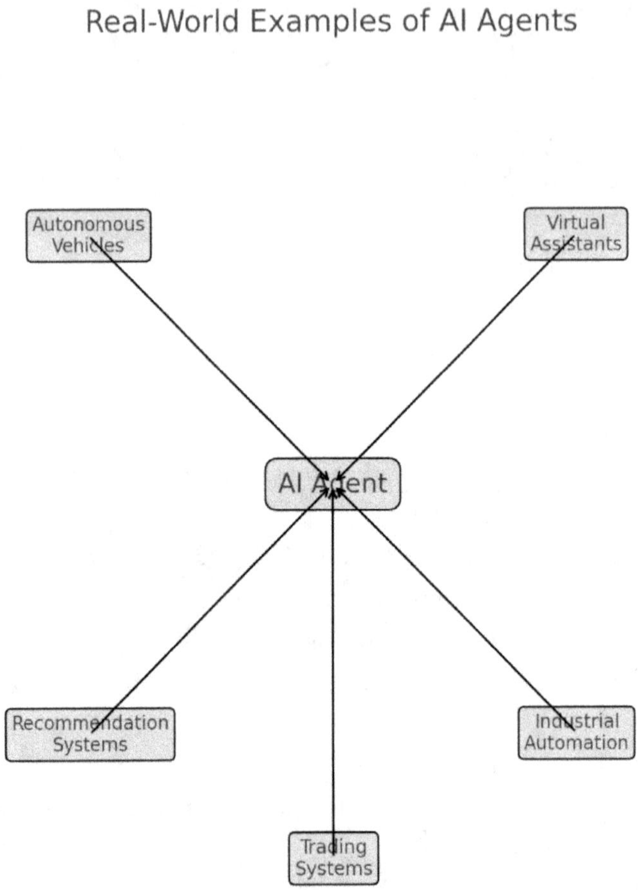

These examples illustrate how the general AI agent architecture adapts to mission-critical tasks in transportation, customer interaction, content delivery, manufacturing, finance, and healthcare. Each domain imposes unique constraints—real-time requirements, safety regulations, or data privacy—shaping the sensors, reasoning methods, and learning strategies an agent employs. Understanding these real-world instances provides a concrete foundation for designing, implementing, and deploying your own AI agents in subsequent chapters.

Chapter 2: Core Concepts and Theory

Intelligent Agent Architectures

The architecture of an intelligent agent defines how it processes information from its environment and determines actions. These architectures range from simple reactive systems to sophisticated planners and learners. Each type suits different kinds of tasks, environments, and levels of complexity.

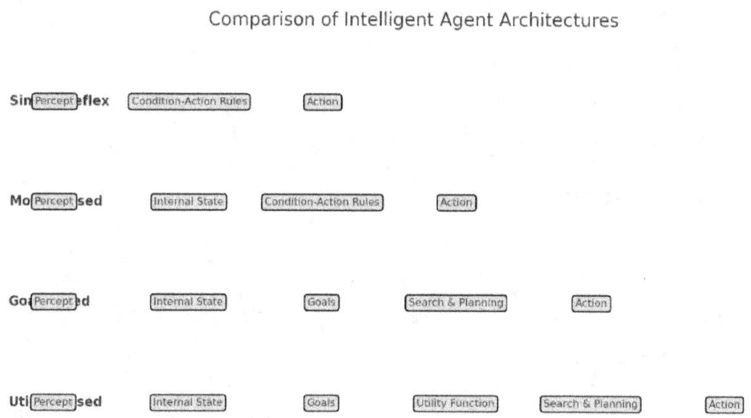

The diagram above illustrates the progression from basic to more advanced agent architectures, with increasing layers of internal representation and decision-making capability.

1. Simple Reflex Agent

Overview:

- Reacts purely based on the current percept using predefined condition-action rules.

- No memory or internal state.
- Effective in fully observable and predictable environments.

Components:

- **Percept → Condition-Action Rules → Action**

Example:

A motion sensor light that turns on when it detects movement.

Limitations:

- Cannot handle partial observability.
- No understanding of long-term consequences or history.

2. Model-Based Reflex Agent

Overview:

- Maintains an **internal state** to keep track of aspects of the world not directly visible.
- Better suited for dynamic and partially observable environments.

Components:

Percept → Internal State → Condition-Action Rules → Action

Example:

A robotic vacuum that remembers the layout of a room and avoids re-cleaning the same area.

Strengths:

- Can infer hidden aspects of the environment.
- More robust than a simple reflex agent.

3. Goal-Based Agent

Overview:

- Makes decisions by considering goals it needs to achieve.
- Uses **search and planning** to determine which actions move it closer to its goals.
- Flexible and adaptable to new situations.

Components:

Percept → Internal State → Goals → Search & Planning → Action

Example:

An autonomous delivery drone that plans a route to deliver a package based on current traffic and weather data.

Advantages:

- Can consider future outcomes.
- Chooses between competing actions based on effectiveness.

4. Utility-Based Agent

Overview:

- Extends goal-based agents by assigning a **utility value** to each possible outcome.
- Chooses the action that maximizes expected utility (e.g., efficiency, safety, profit).
- Helps manage trade-offs between multiple goals.

Components:

Percept → Internal State → Goals → Utility Function → Search & Planning → Action

Example:

A self-driving car that balances speed, safety, and passenger comfort to decide how to drive.

Benefits:

- More nuanced and informed decision-making.
- Optimizes behavior rather than just achieving a goal.

Summary:

Architecture	Memory	Goal-Directed	Optimization	Example Use Case
Simple Reflex	✗	✗	✗	Light switch, alarm system
Model-Based	✓	✗	✗	Cleaning robot, simple game agent
Goal-Based	✓	✓	✗	Delivery drone, search bot
Utility-Based	✓	✓	✓	Autonomous vehicle, financial agent

As we move from simple to utility-based architectures, agents gain more reasoning power, flexibility, and the ability to operate in more complex, uncertain environments. These architectures form the foundation upon which real-world AI systems are built.

Agent Environments

Understanding the environment in which an AI agent operates is crucial to designing effective systems. Environments vary in predictability, complexity, and structure, and these differences directly influence the type of agent architecture required.

Agent Environment Classifications

Deterministic	Next state is fully determined by current state and action.
Stochastic	Next state involves some randomness or uncertainty.
Static	Environment does not change unless affected by the agent.
Dynamic	Environment may change on its own while the agent is deliberating.
Discrete	Finite number of percepts, actions, and states.
Continuous	Infinite possible states, actions, or percepts (e.g., real-valued inputs).

The classification of environments helps us define the challenges an agent faces and tailor its capabilities accordingly. The diagram above outlines six common ways to characterize environments.

1. Deterministic vs. Stochastic

Deterministic Environment:

- **Definition**: The outcome of every action is predictable.
- **Implication**: An agent can rely on fixed rules or models to determine the next state.
- **Example**: A board game like chess (assuming no time limits or outside interference).

Stochastic Environment:

- **Definition**: The same action in the same state can lead to different outcomes.

- **Implication**: The agent must deal with uncertainty and often use probabilistic reasoning or learning.
- **Example**: A robot navigating through a noisy environment with unpredictable obstacles (e.g., moving people).

2. Static vs. Dynamic

Static Environment:

- **Definition**: The environment does not change while the agent is deciding what to do.
- **Implication**: Simpler for agent design; no need to rush decision-making.
- **Example**: Solving a mathematical equation, image recognition, or batch data processing.

Dynamic Environment:

- **Definition**: The environment can change while the agent is thinking or acting.
- **Implication**: The agent must respond quickly or continuously re-evaluate its plans.
- **Example**: Autonomous driving, where other vehicles and pedestrians create a constantly changing environment.

3. Discrete vs. Continuous

Discrete Environment:

- **Definition**: The state space, actions, and percepts are countable and distinct.
- **Implication**: Often easier to model with logical or rule-based approaches.
- **Example**: A turn-based game like Sudoku or tic-tac-toe.

Continuous Environment:

- **Definition**: States, actions, or percepts can take on a range of real values.
- **Implication**: Requires mathematical models, numerical techniques, or deep learning for processing.
- **Example**: A drone flying through 3D space with continuous speed and angle controls.

Summary Table:

Property	Description	Example	Agent Implication
Deterministic	Predictable outcome from each action	Chess	Can rely on planning
Stochastic	Outcomes are uncertain or probabilistic	Stock market	Needs probabilistic reasoning or learning
Static	Does not change unless acted on	Puzzle game	No urgency in decision-making
Dynamic	Changes independent of the agent	Autonomous driving	Requires real-time responses
Discrete	Finite states and actions	Board games	Easier to handle using logic/rules
Continuous	Infinite or real-valued states and actions	Robot control, climate modeling	Requires approximation and computation

Why It Matters

An agent's success depends not just on how it reasons and acts, but also on how well its design fits the environment it operates in. For example:

- A model-free reflex agent might work fine in a static, deterministic game.
- A learning agent is necessary for a dynamic, stochastic environment like financial forecasting.

Understanding environment characteristics helps you anticipate design challenges and choose the right agent architecture, planning algorithms, and learning models. This foundation is essential for real-world deployment and high-performance AI systems

Perception, Reasoning, Action, and Learning in AI Agents

An intelligent agent is defined not just by what it does, but by how it processes information. The cognitive cycle of an AI agent can be broken down into four core functions: **Perception**, **Reasoning**, **Action**, and **Learning**. Together, these components define the agent's ability to function in complex, dynamic environments.

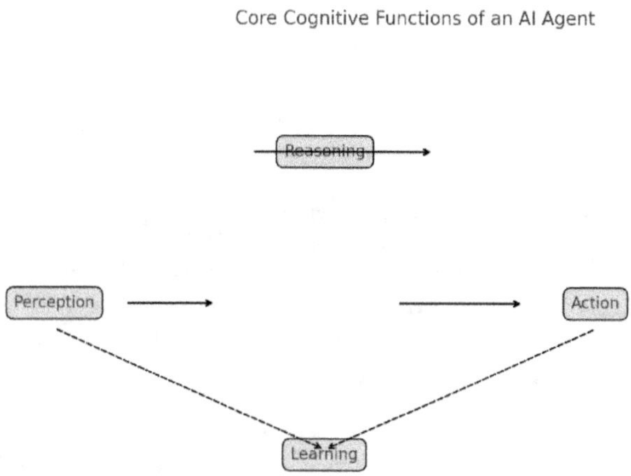

The diagram above illustrates this functional loop: an agent senses its surroundings (Perception), decides what to do (Reasoning), interacts with the environment (Action), and uses feedback to improve over time (Learning).

1. Perception

Perception is the process by which an agent gathers information from its environment using sensors or input data sources.

- **Examples**:
  - A camera feeding image data to a vision model.
  - A chatbot receiving text input from a user.
  - A stock trading agent processing market feeds.

Output: A structured representation of the environment (e.g., objects, positions, context).

Challenges:

- Partial observability

- Noisy or incomplete data
- Real-time constraints

2. Reasoning

Reasoning is the decision-making core of the agent. It takes perceptual inputs and determines what action to take based on the agent's goals, rules, or learned models.

- **Types of Reasoning**:
  - Rule-based (if–then logic)
  - Search-based (A*, depth-first, breadth-first)
  - Probabilistic (Bayesian inference)
  - Machine learning-based (e.g., neural networks, decision trees)

Output: A decision or plan, such as "turn left" or "respond with greeting."

Challenges:

- Balancing speed and accuracy
- Handling uncertainty
- Multi-step planning and goal evaluation

3. Action

Action is how the agent affects its environment based on reasoning. The agent uses actuators (for physical agents) or APIs/output functions (for software agents) to execute decisions.

- **Examples**:
  - A robot arm moving to pick up an object.
  - A drone adjusting altitude.

- A virtual assistant sending a calendar invite.

Output: A tangible effect or output, observable in the environment.

Challenges:

- Real-time execution
- Hardware limitations
- Safety and fail-safes

4. Learning

Learning allows an agent to adapt over time. It improves performance by analyzing outcomes and adjusting future behavior based on feedback.

- **Types of Learning**:
  - Supervised learning: learns from labeled data.
  - Unsupervised learning: finds patterns in unlabeled data.
  - Reinforcement learning: learns by interacting with the environment and receiving rewards or penalties.

Input: Data from perception or results of past actions.

Output: Updated models, rules, or decision policies.

Challenges:

- Avoiding overfitting or underfitting
- Ensuring stability while adapting
- Gathering sufficient and relevant data

Interaction Among Components

As shown in the diagram:

- **Perception** feeds into **Reasoning**, which determines **Action**.
- **Learning** improves both **Perception** and **Action** over time, shown by dashed arrows indicating feedback loops.

This continuous cycle is what makes AI agents autonomous, adaptable, and capable of operating in dynamic real-world environments.

Summary

Function	Role in Agent	Real-World Example
Perception	Sensing input	Image recognition, voice input processing
Reasoning	Decision-making	Route planning, conversation flow control
Action	Executing	Moving, speaking, typing, trading
Learning	Improving	Updating model weights, refining behavior

Together, these four pillars define not just how an agent works, but how it evolves. Mastering them is key to designing capable and intelligent AI systems.

Rationality and Optimality in Decision-Making

A central aspect of AI agent design is how decisions are made. While we aim for optimal behavior, real-world constraints often force a trade-off, leading us to the concept of **rationality**.

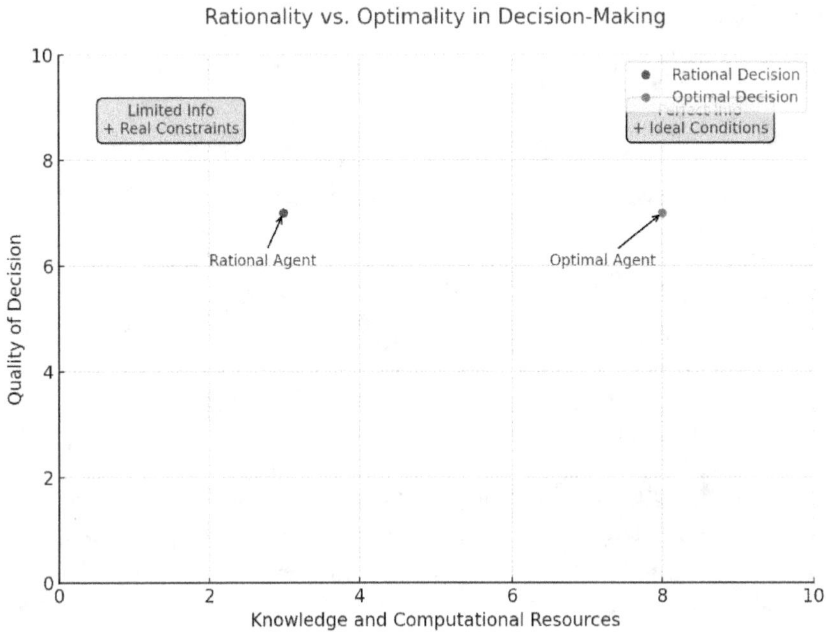

The chart above illustrates the distinction between rational and optimal decisions across axes of knowledge/resources and decision quality.

What Is Rationality?

Rationality refers to an agent's ability to make the best decision it can, given:

- The information it currently has
- Its knowledge of the environment
- Its time and computational constraints

A **rational agent** doesn't always choose the globally best action (i.e., the optimal one), but it always chooses the best possible action under the circumstances.

Key Characteristics:

- Goal-oriented
- Considers available evidence
- Makes decisions with bounded resources

Example:
A navigation system with outdated traffic data may route you through slower streets. While suboptimal, it's rational because it's the best choice given the information it had.

What Is Optimality?

Optimality refers to the best possible action or outcome based on complete knowledge and infinite resources. An **optimal agent** always finds the best path, solution, or answer, assuming perfect conditions.

Example:
An AI chess engine running on supercomputers, with full lookahead to every possible outcome, could make an optimal move every time.

Rationality vs. Optimality: The Practical Difference

Aspect	Rational Agent	Optimal Agent
Knowledge	Limited	Complete
Resources	Bounded (CPU, memory, time)	Unlimited
Decision Quality	Best achievable under the constraints	Best possible in absolute terms
Real-world Fit	High	Rare
Example	Online recommendation system	Exhaustive planner with perfect foresight

Why Rationality Matters More in AI

Real-world agents operate under **uncertainty** and **resource limitations**. For example:

- A robot can't consider every possible trajectory—it has to choose a feasible one quickly.
- A chatbot can't evaluate every response in existence—it must pick the most reasonable one based on training and time limits.

Therefore, in AI system design, **bounded rationality** (a term from cognitive science) is often more relevant than optimality. We aim for agents that:

- React in real-time
- Learn and adapt

- Work with noisy or incomplete data
- Operate safely and effectively under constraints

Summary

- **Optimality** is a theoretical benchmark: perfect action from perfect information.
- **Rationality** is the practical goal: doing the best you can with what you've got.
- **Smart AI design** isn't about chasing perfect decisions—it's about maximizing performance within real limits.

As we build more advanced agents, understanding this distinction helps manage expectations and guides the use of algorithms like heuristics, approximations, and reinforcement learning in practical systems.

Chapter 3: Essential AI Technologies and Algorithms

Search Algorithms

Search algorithms are fundamental tools in the design of intelligent agents, enabling them to navigate decision spaces, find optimal paths, and solve problems. Whether an agent is plotting a path across a map, solving a puzzle, or making a series of strategic decisions, search forms the backbone of intelligent reasoning.

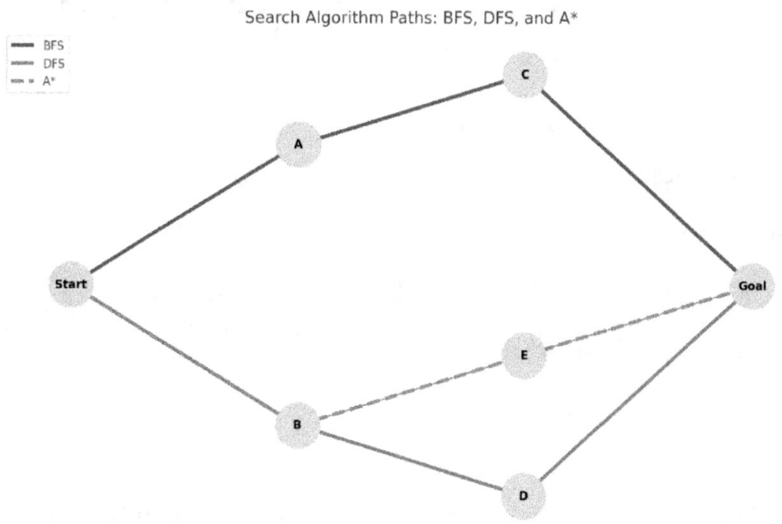

The diagram above illustrates how three common search algorithms - **Breadth-First Search (BFS)**, **Depth-First Search (DFS)**, and **A*** - explore a search space differently, using a simplified graph.

1. Breadth-First Search (BFS)

Overview:

BFS explores the shallowest nodes first—working level by level from the start node. It guarantees the shortest path in terms of the number of steps (if all actions have equal cost).

How It Works:

- Uses a queue (FIFO) to track unexplored nodes.
- Expands all immediate neighbors before moving deeper.

Characteristics:

- **Complete**: Will find a solution if one exists.
- **Optimal**: Yes, for uniform step costs.
- **Time & Space Complexity**: O(b^d), where b is the branching factor and d is depth.

Use Case:

- Finding the shortest path in unweighted graphs or grids.

In the Graph:

- The blue path shows BFS from "Start" to "Goal" via nodes A → C.

2. Depth-First Search (DFS)

Overview:

DFS dives as deep as possible along a branch before backtracking. It uses a stack (LIFO) structure, either explicitly or through recursion.

How It Works:

- Explores one branch fully before moving to another.
- Can get stuck in deep or infinite paths unless depth-limited.

Characteristics:

- **Complete**: Only in finite graphs or with depth limits.
- **Optimal**: No—it may find suboptimal solutions first.

- **Time & Space Complexity**: O(b^d), but lower space use than BFS.

Use Case:

- Games, puzzles, or when solutions are deep and memory is limited.

In the Graph:

- The green path shows DFS going deep into the path B → D → Goal.

3. A* Search

Overview:

A* is an informed search algorithm that uses heuristics to find the most promising path. It combines the cost to reach a node (g(n)) with a heuristic estimate of the cost to reach the goal (h(n)).

Formula:

$f(n) = g(n) + h(n)$

Characteristics:

- **Complete**: Yes, if the heuristic is admissible.
- **Optimal**: Yes, with admissible and consistent heuristics.
- **Time & Space Complexity**: Depends on heuristic quality, worst case O(b^d).

Use Case:

- Route planning, AI in games, real-time strategy decisions.

In the Graph:

- The red dashed path shows A* selecting the B → E route, assuming E → Goal has a lower heuristic cost.

4. Heuristic Search

A* is a heuristic search, but the term also refers to any method that uses problem-specific knowledge to guide exploration:

- **Greedy Best-First Search** uses only h(n) (ignores cost so far).
- **A*** balances past and estimated future cost.

Good heuristics:

- Are problem-specific
- Must be admissible (never overestimate)
- Should be consistent (obey triangle inequality)

Summary Comparison

Algorithm	Strategy	Optimal	Complete	Uses Heuristic	Best For
BFS	Level-order	Yes	Yes	No	Shortest path in unweighted graphs
DFS	Deep-first	No	Yes*	No	Deep solutions, low memory
A*	Cost + Heuristic	Yes	Yes	Yes	Efficient, informed pathfinding

Choosing the right search algorithm depends on your problem constraints - whether you're optimizing for speed, memory, or solution quality. In practice, hybrid methods and customized heuristics often yield the best results, especially in domains like robotics, games, and logistics where efficient pathfinding is mission-critical.

Decision-Making Under Uncertainty

Focus: MDPs and POMDPs

In real-world environments, AI agents often face uncertainty. They may not know exactly what will happen as a result of an action or may not have full visibility of the world around them. This is where **Markov Decision Processes (MDPs)** and **Partially Observable Markov Decision Processes (POMDPs)** come into play.

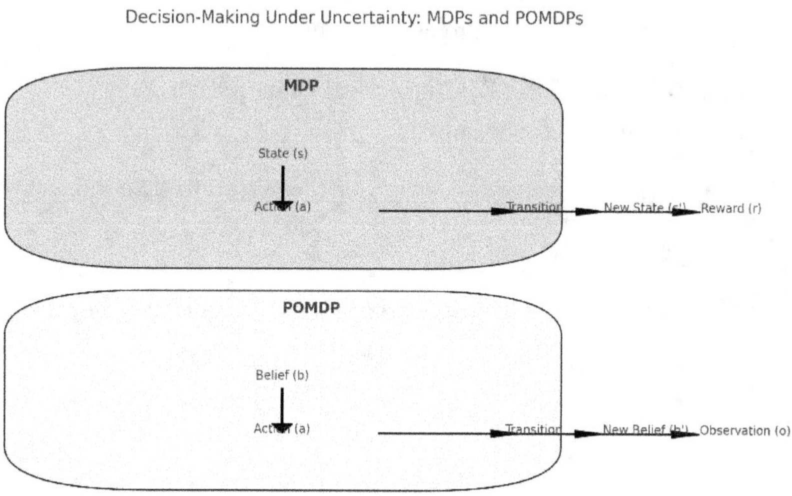

The diagram above contrasts the structures of MDPs and POMDPs - two powerful models that guide intelligent decision-making under uncertainty.

What is an MDP?

Markov Decision Process (MDP)

An MDP is a mathematical framework for modeling decision-making where outcomes are partly random and partly under the control of an agent.

MDP Components:

- **States (s)**: The current configuration of the environment.
- **Actions (a)**: Choices the agent can make.
- **Transition Function (T)**: Probability distribution over next states, given current state and action.
- **Reward Function (R)**: Numerical value received after transitioning to a new state.
- **Policy (π)**: A strategy that defines the action to take in each state.

Key Properties:

- **Markov Property**: Future state depends only on the current state and action, not on prior history.
- **Fully Observable**: The agent knows the current state with certainty.

Applications:

- Robot path planning
- Game playing (e.g., chess, Go)
- Inventory control systems

What is a POMDP?

Partially Observable Markov Decision Process (POMDP)

A POMDP extends the MDP framework to environments where the agent cannot fully observe the state of the environment.

POMDP Components:

- **Belief (b)**: A probability distribution over possible states (agent's internal estimation).
- **Actions (a)**: Same as in MDP.
- **Transition Function (T)**: Governs how the environment evolves.
- **Observation Function (O)**: Probability of seeing an observation given the true state.
- **Reward Function (R)**: As in MDP, based on the underlying state and action.
- **Policy (π)**: Maps beliefs (not states) to actions.

Key Differences from MDP:

- **Partial Observability**: The agent receives **observations**, not states.
- **Belief State**: Decision-making is based on a belief about the state, not the actual state.

Applications:

- Medical diagnosis (where symptoms are indirect evidence)
- Assistive robots (with sensor noise)
- Speech and vision systems

Visual Explanation of Flow

In an MDP:

1. The agent observes the exact state s.

2. Chooses action a.
3. Transitions to a new state s' with reward r.
4. This loop repeats as the agent follows a policy to maximize total expected rewards.

In a POMDP:

1. The agent maintains a belief b (a guess of the true state).
2. Takes action a.
3. Transitions to a new hidden state and receives an observation o.
4. Updates its belief b' based on o and continues.

Solving MDPs vs. POMDPs

Method	Solving Approach	Computational Complexity
MDP	Dynamic Programming, Value Iteration, Policy Iteration	Moderate
POMDP	Belief-space Search, Point-Based Approximations	High (PSPACE-hard)

Summary:

Feature	MDP	POMDP
Observability	Full	Partial
Decision Basis	Actual state	Belief about state
Environment Model	Transition + reward	Transition + observation + reward
Example Use Case	Route planning with a map	Navigation with fog or noisy GPS

MDPs and POMDPs offer structured, principled approaches to decision-making under uncertainty. As environments grow more complex and less predictable, mastering these models becomes essential for building truly intelligent agents that reason under real-world conditions. In practice, they form the backbone of many advanced AI systems - from adaptive robotics to interactive recommendation engines and autonomous vehicles.

Reinforcement Learning (Q-Learning, Deep RL)

Reinforcement Learning (RL) is a foundational approach to building AI agents that learn through interaction with their environment. Unlike supervised learning, which learns from labeled examples, RL teaches agents through **trial and error**, using rewards and penalties as feedback. It's particularly useful when the correct action isn't known ahead of time but must be discovered through experience.

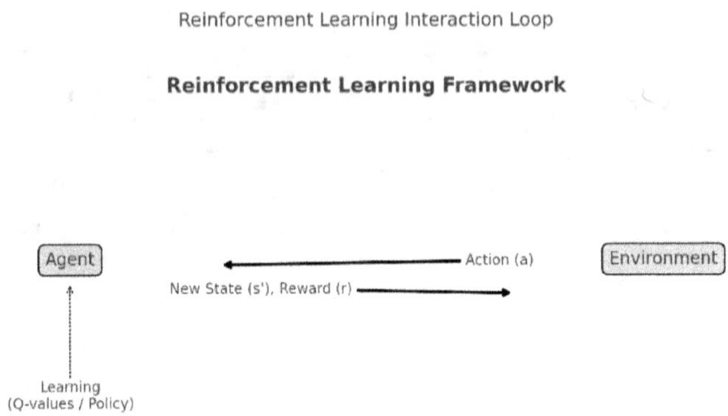

The diagram above illustrates the RL loop, showing how an agent interacts continuously with its environment to improve over time.

Core Reinforcement Learning Framework

Reinforcement Learning is built on the following key components:

- **Agent**: The learner or decision-maker.
- **Environment**: The system the agent interacts with.
- **State (s)**: A representation of the environment at a given time.
- **Action (a)**: A choice made by the agent.
- **Reward (r)**: Feedback signal indicating the value of the outcome.
- **Policy (π)**: Strategy the agent uses to decide actions.
- **Value Function (V or Q)**: Estimate of expected long-term rewards.

At each step, the agent:

1. Observes the current state s.

2. Chooses an action a using its policy.
3. Receives a reward r and transitions to a new state s'.
4. Updates its internal model (e.g., value function or policy).

Q-Learning: A Model-Free RL Algorithm

Overview:

Q-Learning is a popular off-policy, model-free algorithm that learns the value of taking a particular action in a given state. It updates estimates using the Bellman Equation.

Update Rule:

$Q(s, a) \leftarrow Q(s, a) + \alpha\, [r + \gamma \max(Q(s', a')) - Q(s, a)]$

- α: Learning rate
- γ: Discount factor for future rewards
- r: Immediate reward
- $\max(Q(s', a'))$: Estimate of optimal future value

Characteristics:

- Does not require a model of the environment
- Proven to converge to the optimal policy with enough exploration
- Suitable for discrete state-action spaces

Example Use Case:

Training a robot to navigate a gridworld or a game AI learning how to score points through exploration.

Deep Reinforcement Learning (Deep RL)

Overview:

Deep RL combines RL principles with deep neural networks to handle high-dimensional or continuous state spaces that traditional Q-Learning cannot manage.

Key Algorithms:

- **Deep Q-Networks (DQN)**: Approximate Q-values using a neural network.
- **Policy Gradient Methods (REINFORCE, PPO)**: Directly optimize the policy using gradient ascent.
- **Actor-Critic Models**: Combine value-based and policy-based methods using two networks—one for the value (critic) and one for the policy (actor).

Advantages:

- Handles images, raw sensor input, and large state spaces
- Learns complex behaviors without manual feature engineering

Example Use Cases:

- Playing Atari games using raw pixels
- Controlling robotic arms in simulation and real environments
- Optimizing resource allocation in data centers

Exploration vs. Exploitation

A core challenge in RL is the balance between:

- **Exploration**: Trying new actions to discover better rewards.
- **Exploitation**: Using known actions that yield high rewards.

Strategies like ε-greedy, Boltzmann exploration, or entropy bonuses help manage this trade-off.

Summary Comparison

Feature	Q-Learning	Deep RL
Input	Discrete states/actions	High-dimensional inputs (e.g., images)
Representation	Q-table	Neural network
Sample Efficiency	Moderate	Low (but scalable)
Complexity	Low	High
Use Case	Grid worlds, games	Robotics, visual input tasks

Reinforcement Learning provides a framework for building agents that learn to make complex decisions autonomously. From Q-learning's simple tabular approach to Deep RL's neural-powered strategies, this area of AI has opened up new frontiers in robotics, gaming, and adaptive control systems. Mastery of RL equips you to create agents that not only act, but also learn and evolve in unpredictable environments.

Planning and Scheduling Algorithms

In AI, **planning** and **scheduling** algorithms enable agents to sequence actions, allocate resources, and optimize workflows to achieve goals. These algorithms are crucial in autonomous systems, robotics, logistics, and any domain where tasks must be executed efficiently under constraints.

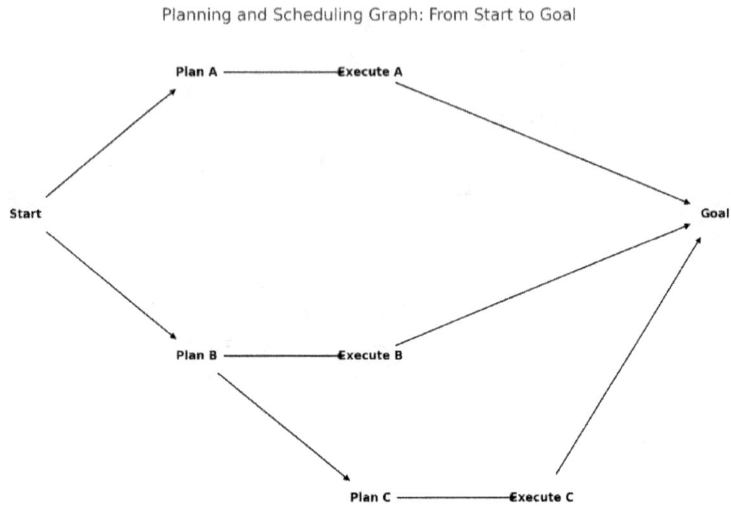

The diagram above shows a **planning graph**, which represents a set of possible plans and execution paths from a starting state to a goal, helping the agent decide on the best route to take.

What Is Planning?

Planning is the process of deciding **what to do** - selecting a sequence of actions that transforms the current state into a desired goal state.

Types of Planning:

1. Classical Planning

- Assumes a known, deterministic, and fully observable environment.
- Operates on symbolic representations (e.g., STRIPS).
- Algorithms:
    - **Forward search (Progression Planning)**: Starts from initial state and moves toward goal.

- **Backward search (Regression Planning)**: Starts from goal and works backward to the start.
- **GraphPlan**: Builds a planning graph of reachable actions and states.

Example: A robot figuring out how to move blocks from one configuration to another.

2. Heuristic Planning

- Uses domain-specific heuristics to estimate the cost to reach the goal.
- Algorithms:
  - **A* for Planning**: Uses heuristic cost estimates to find the optimal path of actions.
  - **HSP, Fast-Downward**: Specialized planners for domain-independent problems.

What Is Scheduling?

Scheduling deals with **when** to do tasks—assigning time and resources to actions or jobs while respecting constraints (time, capacity, dependencies).

Types of Scheduling:

1. Job-Shop Scheduling

- Assigns tasks to resources (like machines) with predefined durations.
- Considers order constraints (e.g., Task B must follow Task A).

2. Temporal Planning

- Extends classical planning to include durations and temporal constraints.

- Requires coordination across tasks with start/end times.

3. Resource-Constrained Scheduling

- Tasks compete for limited resources (e.g., robots, CPU, fuel).
- Must optimize usage and avoid conflicts.

Common Planning & Scheduling Algorithms

Algorithm	Purpose	Strengths
A* Search	Path or action planning	Optimal if heuristic is admissible
STRIPS	Symbolic action planning	Simple and widely supported
GraphPlan	Parallelizable action plans	Efficient for large problem spaces
CSP (Constraint Satisfaction)	Task allocation and constraint enforcement	Great for resource-based scheduling
PERT/CPM	Task duration management	Useful in project scheduling scenarios

Real-World Applications

- **Robotics**: Path and task planning for multi-step missions.
- **Logistics**: Fleet dispatching, delivery routing.
- **Manufacturing**: Scheduling of jobs on machines.
- **Cloud Computing**: Assigning tasks to VMs with constraints.
- **Autonomous Vehicles**: Route planning under traffic conditions.

Diagram Explanation

In the planning graph above:

- The agent starts at a decision point (Start).
- Multiple planning branches (Plan A, Plan B, Plan C) are available.
- Each plan leads to a specific execution path (Execute A, Execute B, Execute C).
- All paths converge on the shared goal (Goal), but with different cost/benefit trade-offs.

This visual structure mirrors how planning algorithms work: by evaluating multiple paths and choosing the most effective one based on rules, heuristics, or learned models.

Summary

Aspect	Planning	Scheduling
Focus	What actions to take	When and how to perform actions
Inputs	Initial state, goal	Tasks, deadlines, resource limits
Output	Action sequence	Timelines, task-resource allocation
Used In	Decision-making, robotics	Resource management, operations

Together, planning and scheduling allow agents to operate not just intelligently, but efficiently and practically - especially in constrained, dynamic, and multi-tasking environments.

Part 2: Building AI Agents from Scratch
Chapter 4: Setting Up Your Environment

Languages: Python, R, and JavaScript

Before building any AI agent, you need a well-configured development environment tailored to the tools and libraries that best suit your goals.

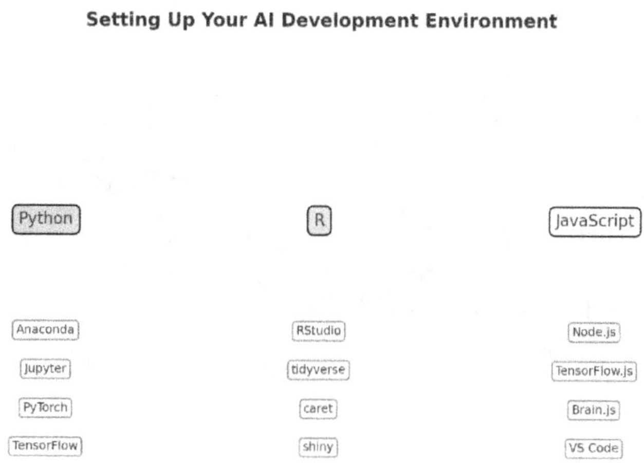

The diagram above outlines three major languages used in AI development - **Python, R**, and **JavaScript** - along with the key libraries and platforms associated with each.

Python: The Most Popular Language for AI

Python is the dominant language for AI development due to its rich ecosystem, ease of use, and extensive support for machine learning and data science.

Tools & Libraries:

- **Anaconda**: A distribution that simplifies Python installation and package management.
- **Jupyter Notebook**: An interactive coding environment ideal for prototyping, visualization, and documentation.
- **PyTorch**: A powerful deep learning framework favored for flexibility and ease of debugging.
- **TensorFlow**: A scalable machine learning platform developed by Google, widely used in both research and production.

Setup Instructions:

1. Install Anaconda.
2. Launch Jupyter via the Anaconda Navigator or command line.
3. Use pip or conda to install packages like tensorflow, torch, scikit-learn.

Ideal For:

- Deep learning models
- Research and experimentation
- Large-scale machine learning systems

R: Built for Statistical Analysis

R is widely used in academia and analytics-heavy fields, offering robust libraries for data manipulation and modeling.

Tools & Libraries:

- **RStudio**: A popular IDE for R development.
- **tidyverse**: A collection of packages for data science (e.g., ggplot2, dplyr, readr).

- **caret**: A package for classification and regression training.
- **shiny**: Enables building interactive web applications using R.

Setup Instructions:

1. Download and install R and RStudio.
2. Use install.packages("tidyverse") to begin setting up your toolkit.

Ideal For:

- Statistical modeling
- Rapid analysis and visualization
- Building data dashboards

🌐 JavaScript: AI in the Browser

JavaScript enables AI directly in the browser or via back-end environments using Node.js. It's perfect for deploying lightweight, interactive agents without server dependencies.

Tools & Libraries:

- **Node.js**: Server-side runtime for JavaScript.
- **TensorFlow.js**: A JavaScript library to run ML models in the browser or on Node.js.
- **Brain.js**: A lightweight library for simple neural networks.
- **VS Code**: A popular and extensible editor for web and server-side development.

Setup Instructions:

1. Install Node.js and VS Code.
2. Use npm install @tensorflow/tfjs or npm install brain.js for ML libraries.

3. Run models directly in the browser or via Node scripts.

Ideal For:

- Interactive web applications
- Client-side inference
- Low-latency applications without server calls

Choosing the Right Tool for the Job

Criteria	Python	R	JavaScript
Ease of Use	High	Medium	High
Best For	General AI & ML	Data analysis	Web-based AI
Community & Support	Very Large	Large	Growing
Learning Curve	Moderate	Moderate	Low

Final Tips

- Use **virtual environments** (venv, conda, or renv) to manage dependencies safely.
- Keep your **IDE consistent** with your language (e.g., Jupyter for Python, RStudio for R, VS Code for JS).
- For multi-language projects (e.g., backend in Python, frontend in JS), use containers like **Docker** for consistent environments.

Setting up your environment correctly is the first step toward building reliable and efficient AI agents. Once you're comfortable with your tools, you'll be ready to move on to implementing your first agent

Essential Libraries and Frameworks

Once your development environment is ready, the next step is choosing the right **libraries and frameworks**. These tools accelerate development by providing optimized, reusable building blocks for tasks like deep learning, reinforcement learning, and neural network inference.

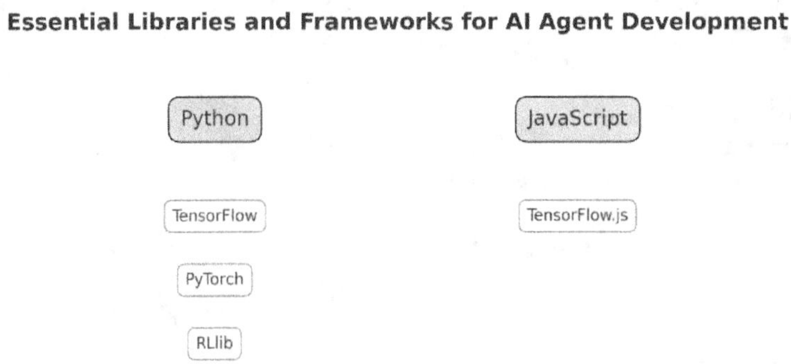

The diagram above highlights key libraries for two popular languages in AI development: **Python** and **JavaScript**.

Python Libraries

Python dominates the AI landscape, and for good reason—it has deep ecosystem support and powerful open-source libraries tailored to different types of AI agents.

1. TensorFlow

- Developed by Google.
- Widely used for building and training neural networks.
- Features:
  - Declarative graph-based computation.
  - GPU acceleration.
  - Compatible with production deployment (via TensorFlow Serving or TensorFlow Lite).
- Ideal For:
  - Deep learning models.
  - Scalable training pipelines.
  - Cross-platform deployment (web, mobile, edge).

2. PyTorch

- Developed by Meta (Facebook).
- Emphasizes ease of use and dynamic computation graphs.
- Features:
  - More "Pythonic" than TensorFlow.
  - Strong support for research and rapid prototyping.
  - Integrated ecosystem: TorchVision, TorchRL, etc.
- Ideal For:
  - Natural language processing.
  - Research-based AI development.
  - Models requiring dynamic architectures.

3. RLlib (from Ray)

- A high-level library for **reinforcement learning**.
- Part of the Ray distributed framework.
- Features:
  - Scales RL training across CPUs and GPUs with minimal code changes.
  - Supports major RL algorithms (PPO, DQN, A3C).
  - Integrates with both TensorFlow and PyTorch.
- Ideal For:
  - Multi-agent simulations.
  - Production-ready RL systems.
  - Large-scale experimentation.

🌐 JavaScript Library

JavaScript is gaining traction in the AI space, especially for deploying models directly in browsers or on lightweight edge devices.

1. TensorFlow.js

- Brings TensorFlow's capabilities to JavaScript.
- Can run models:
  - In the browser using WebGL.
  - On Node.js servers.
- Features:
  - Real-time interactivity with web applications.
  - Train and infer models directly in the browser.

   - Compatible with existing Python-trained models.
- Ideal For:
   - Browser-based AI (e.g., webcam apps, live image classification).
   - Educational demos and interactive AI tools.
   - Lightweight and cross-platform applications.

Choosing the Right Tool

Use Case	Recommended Library
Research and prototyping (Python)	PyTorch
Scalable production systems	TensorFlow or RLlib
Reinforcement learning agents	RLlib
AI in the browser	TensorFlow.js
Cross-platform model deployment	TensorFlow

Each library serves a specific role:

- Use **PyTorch** for flexibility and experimentation.
- Choose **TensorFlow** for robust, production-grade pipelines.
- Leverage **RLlib** for managing complex, multi-agent environments.
- Use **TensorFlow.js** when deploying AI models in the browser without a server.

Selecting the right library sets the foundation for how quickly, effectively, and scalably you can build your AI agent - so it's worth making an informed decision based on your goals.

Chapter 5: Basic Agent Implementation

Creating a Simple Reflex Agent

A **Simple Reflex Agent** is the most basic type of AI agent. It makes decisions solely based on the current percept - what it senses at the moment - without any memory of past events or consideration of future consequences.

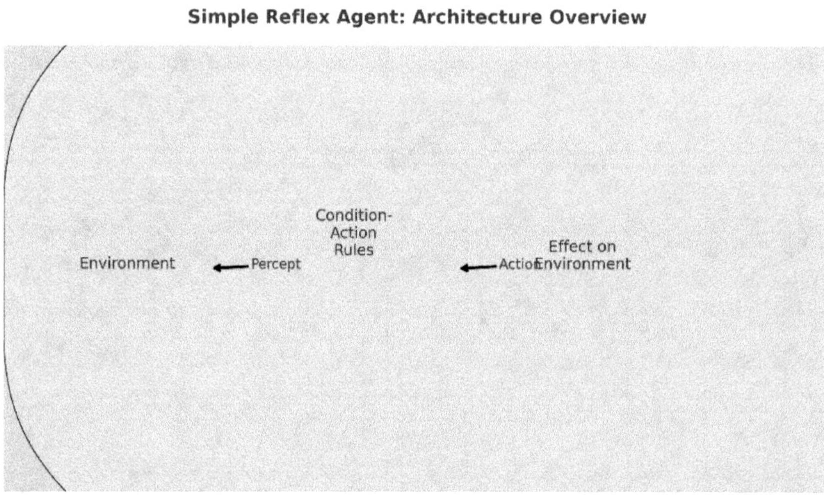

The diagram above illustrates the structure of a simple reflex agent. It's a straightforward system where percepts (inputs from the environment) trigger predefined condition–action rules, leading directly to an output or action.

🔧 How It Works

1. Percept (Input)

The agent senses the current state of the environment through sensors. This input is referred to as a **percept**.

2. Condition-Action Rules

The core of the agent is a simple set of **if–then** rules:

```
if condition:
    do action
```

These rules form the decision logic. The agent does not store any history or maintain an internal model of the environment.

3. Action (Output)

Based on the matched condition, the agent performs a specific action. This is done via actuators or some defined interface that interacts with the environment.

🧠 Simple Code Example (Python)

Here's a basic example of a reflex agent that controls a vacuum robot:

```
def reflex_vacuum_agent(percept):
    if percept == "dirty":
        return "clean"
    elif percept == "clean":
        return "move"
```

- If the environment is dirty, the agent will clean.
- If it's already clean, it moves to the next area.

✅ Advantages

- **Fast and efficient**: No need for heavy computation or memory.
- **Easy to implement**: Works well for fully observable, simple environments.

❌ Limitations

- **No memory**: It can't learn or adapt from past experiences.
- **No planning**: It only handles immediate situations, not long-term goals.
- **Fails in complex or partially observable environments**.

When to Use

Simple reflex agents are ideal when:

- The environment is fully observable and predictable.
- The tasks are repetitive and have straightforward rules.
- You want a quick prototype for basic behaviors.

Examples in the real world:

- Light sensors that switch on when it's dark.
- Basic thermostat systems.
- Obstacle-avoiding bots in fixed mazes.

Summary

Feature	**Simple Reflex Agent**
Memory	❌ None
Learning Capability	❌ None
Speed	✅ Very Fast
Complexity Handling	❌ Very Limited
Ideal Use Case	Fully observable environments

By starting with a simple reflex agent, you lay the foundation for more advanced agent types. Understanding this model helps you grasp how input-to-output loops work in AI and sets the stage for building agents with memory, goals, and learning in the next steps.

Building Rule-Based Agents

A **rule-based agent** is an advancement over a simple reflex agent. It still relies on condition–action logic but introduces a structured rule base and decision mechanism. These agents can handle a wider range of inputs and support more complex behaviors by evaluating a **set of rules** to choose the appropriate action.

Rule-Based Agent: Logical Flow Diagram

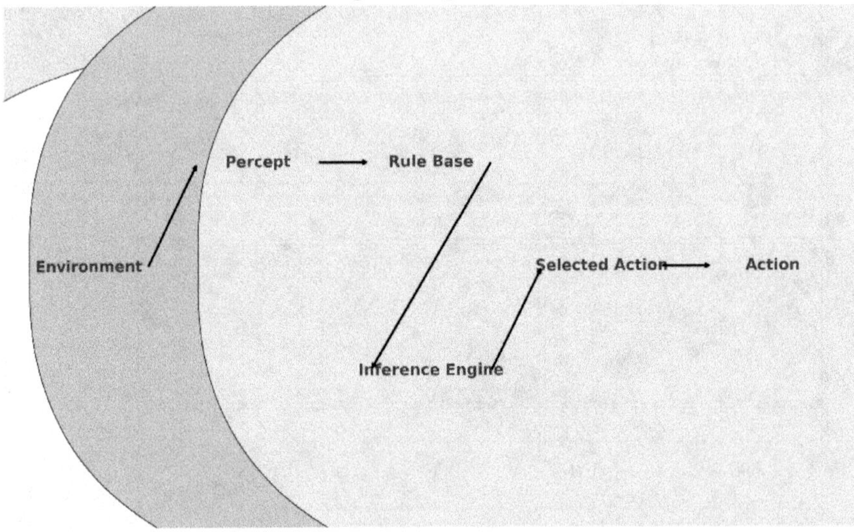

The diagram above illustrates the architecture of a rule-based agent, showing how percepts from the environment are matched against a rule base through an inference engine that selects the best action.

🧠 How Rule-Based Agents Work

1. Perception

The agent receives **input** from the environment—this could be sensor data, user input, or system states.

2. Rule Base

A collection of condition–action pairs, often expressed as **if–then rules**:

```
if condition_1:
    do action_1
elif condition_2:
    do action_2
```

This allows the agent to reason about various scenarios by matching percepts to rules.

3. Inference Engine

This component matches incoming percepts against the rules in the rule base and selects the most relevant action(s) to execute. In some designs, it may:

- Prioritize rules
- Handle conflicts
- Chain rules for multi-step logic

4. Action

The agent executes the chosen action to influence the environment.

🔧 Simple Python Example

```
def rule_based_agent(percept):
    rules = {
        "obstacle": "turn",
        "dirty": "clean",
        "clean": "move"
```

```
}
return rules.get(percept, "wait")
```

- If the percept is "obstacle", the agent turns.
- If "dirty", it cleans.
- If "clean", it moves.
- If unknown, it waits.

✅ **Advantages**

- **Modular**: Easy to extend by adding new rules.
- **Interpretable**: Logic is explicit and transparent.
- **Versatile**: Can be used for many structured decision-making tasks.

❌ **Limitations**

- **Scalability**: As the rule base grows, it becomes harder to manage.
- **Static Knowledge**: Rules don't adapt or learn.
- **Brittleness**: Performance degrades in dynamic or uncertain environments.

🤖 **Use Cases**

- Chatbots with predefined responses.
- Customer service automation.
- Industrial control systems.
- Game AI for deterministic responses.

Summary

Feature	Rule-Based Agent
Memory	Indirect (via rule coverage)
Learning Capability	❌ Not built-in
Decision Strategy	Rule matching with inference logic
Adaptability	❌ Limited
Transparency	✅ High (easy to audit and modify)
Best Use Case	Well-defined, rule-governed environments

Rule-based agents represent a critical stepping stone between basic reactive systems and adaptive, learning-based AI. They are powerful for domains where the logic is well understood and can be explicitly encoded, offering clarity and control in agent behavior.

Hands-on Example: Simple Game-Playing Agent

A game-playing agent is a great hands-on way to understand AI principles in action. This type of agent perceives the current state of a game, evaluates possible moves, selects the most promising one, and takes action. It repeats this cycle until the game concludes.

Simple Game-Playing Agent: Decision Flow

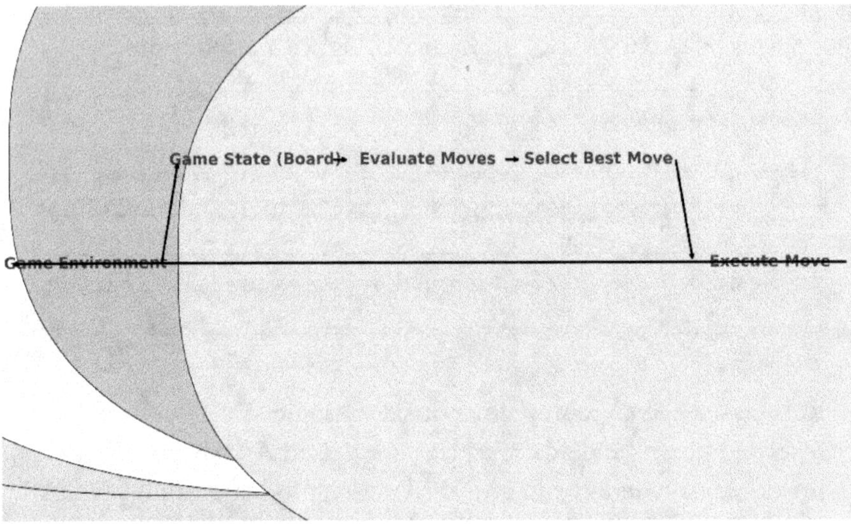

The diagram above illustrates a simple decision-making flow of such an agent, ideal for turn-based games like tic-tac-toe, checkers, or simplified strategy games.

🧠 What Does the Agent Do?

1. Game Environment

The game environment controls the rules, tracks the game state, and applies actions. It interacts with the agent to provide current game conditions and accepts moves from the agent.

2. Game State (Board)

The agent receives the current state of the game—usually represented as a data structure like a grid or array. For example, in tic-tac-toe, this could be a 3x3 matrix.

3. Evaluate Moves

The agent examines all legal moves it can make from the current state. For each move, it simulates the outcome and evaluates it using a scoring function.

4. Select Best Move

After evaluating all options, the agent picks the move with the highest score based on its strategy. This could be:

- A fixed set of rules (rule-based strategy)
- A heuristic (simple evaluation logic)
- A search algorithm (like Minimax)

5. Execute Move

The agent plays its move in the environment. This updates the game state and passes control to the opponent or triggers the next cycle of evaluation.

The process loops until the game ends in a win, loss, or draw.

Sample Python Implementation: Tic-Tac-Toe Agent

```
def evaluate(board):

    # Simple scoring logic: +1 for win, -1 for loss, 0 for draw or ongoing

    # This is a placeholder; real logic would check all rows, cols, diagonals

    return 0
```

```
def get_legal_moves(board):
    return [i for i, v in enumerate(board) if v == " "]


def agent_move(board, symbol):
    best_score = float('-inf')
    best_move = None
    for move in get_legal_moves(board):
        board[move] = symbol
        score = evaluate(board)
        board[move] = " "  # Undo move
        if score > best_score:
            best_score = score
            best_move = move
    return best_move
```

✅ **Strengths of a Simple Game-Playing Agent**

- **Fast and predictable**
- **Easy to debug and extend**
- **Great for learning AI basics**

❌ **Limitations**

- Limited strategic depth unless enhanced with learning or search.
- Cannot adapt to new game types without reprogramming.

Next Steps

To make this agent smarter:

- Add search (Minimax with Alpha-Beta Pruning)
- Integrate reinforcement learning (e.g., Q-learning)
- Build an opponent model

Summary

Component	Role in Agent
Game Environment	Governs rules and state transitions
Game State	Current snapshot of board or game scenario
Evaluate Moves	Analyze possible future outcomes
Select Best Move	Choose the optimal action
Execute Move	Apply the decision and update the game

This foundational pattern is used in many intelligent systems, from board game agents to video game NPCs. It's simple, yet powerful enough to grow into more advanced forms of AI.

Chapter 6: Advanced Agent Architectures

Implementing Model-Based and Goal-Driven Agents

As AI agents grow more capable, they must move beyond simple reflexes and incorporate deeper reasoning about the world. Two advanced forms - **model-based** and **goal-driven** agents - offer just that.

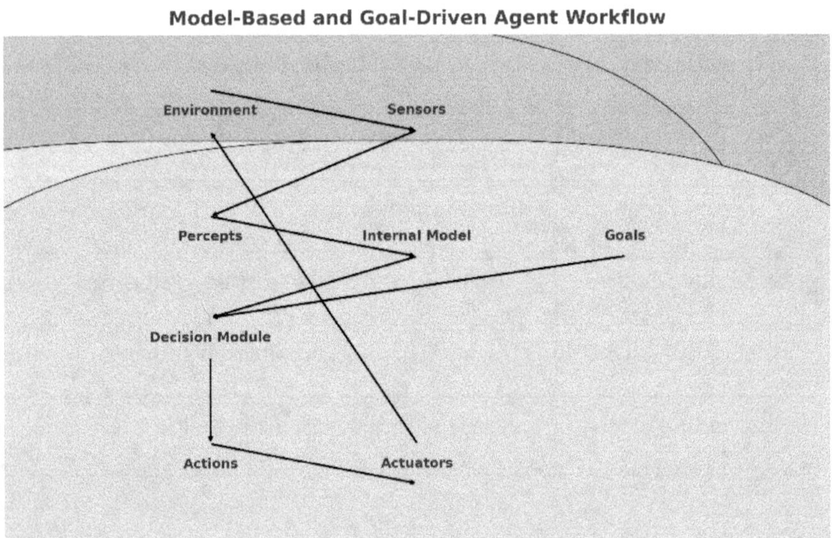

The diagram above illustrates the internal architecture of a model-based, goal-driven agent. Unlike reflex agents, this type of agent maintains an internal model of the environment and chooses actions strategically to achieve defined goals.

What Is a Model-Based Agent?

A **model-based agent** maintains a representation of how the world works. Instead of reacting to inputs in isolation, it infers hidden aspects of the environment using both current percepts and past experiences.

Key Features:

- **Internal Model**: Captures the structure of the environment, such as object positions, physics, or other agents' behaviors.
- **Percept Integration**: New percepts update the model, refining the agent's understanding of the world.
- **Forward Simulation**: Can simulate potential outcomes of actions before choosing one.

🎯 What Is a Goal-Driven Agent?

A **goal-driven agent** acts to achieve specific outcomes rather than simply reacting to conditions. It reasons about how to reach a goal and selects actions based on a **plan**, not just a condition-action rule.

Key Features:

- **Goal Formulation**: A clearly defined end state or set of conditions to reach.
- **Deliberation**: Evaluates multiple potential actions or plans.
- **Decision Making**: Chooses actions that increase the likelihood of achieving the goal.

🔄 Agent Architecture Overview

The chart above breaks the agent into the following components:

1. Environment

The world in which the agent operates. It provides percepts and is modified by actions.

2. Sensors

Capture data from the environment and pass it to the agent.

3. Percepts

The immediate observations or inputs (e.g., camera image, sensor reading).

4. Internal Model

An ongoing representation of the environment. This allows the agent to infer unobservable facts and maintain state over time.

5. Goals

A set of desired states that the agent is trying to achieve.

6. Decision Module

This is where reasoning happens. It uses the internal model and goals to evaluate which action should be taken. Techniques here can include:

- Search and planning (e.g., A*, STRIPS)
- Constraint satisfaction
- Logical inference

7. Actions

The agent's selected response, determined through planning or evaluation.

8. Actuators

Components that interact with the environment (e.g., motors, speech output, API calls).

🔧 Python Example Sketch

```
class GoalDrivenAgent:
    def __init__(self, model, goals):
        self.model = model
        self.goals = goals
    def perceive(self, percept):
        self.model.update(percept)
    def decide(self):
        plan = self.plan_toward_goals()
        return plan[0] if plan else None
    def plan_toward_goals(self):
        # Mock planning logic
        return ["move_to_target", "interact"]
# Example usage:
agent = GoalDrivenAgent(model=WorldModel(),
goals=["reach_target"])
agent.perceive({"location": "start"})
action = agent.decide()
```

✅ Benefits of Model-Based, Goal-Driven Agents

- **Strategic**: Capable of planning and adapting.
- **Scalable**: Suitable for complex domains like robotics, logistics, and games.
- **Flexible**: Can pursue dynamic goals and recover from failure.

❌ **Challenges**

- **More complex to implement**
- **Requires accurate modeling**
- **Computationally intensive**

Summary

Feature	Reflex Agent	Model-Based Agent	Goal-Driven Agent
Memory	❌ None	✅ Internal state	✅ Internal state + goals
Future Planning	❌ None	✅ Limited simulation	✅ Full goal-based planning
Complexity Handling	❌ Poor	✅ Moderate	✅ High
Adaptability	❌ Low	✅ Higher	✅ Dynamic, goal-sensitive

Advanced architectures like these are critical for agents that must navigate uncertainty, reason over time, and make intelligent choices aligned with long-term objectives.

Creating a Utility-Based Decision-Making System

A **utility-based agent** is one of the most sophisticated decision-making architectures in AI. Rather than merely reacting to rules or pursuing predefined goals, it evaluates a set of possible actions and chooses the one that maximizes its **utility**—a measure of how desirable a given outcome is.

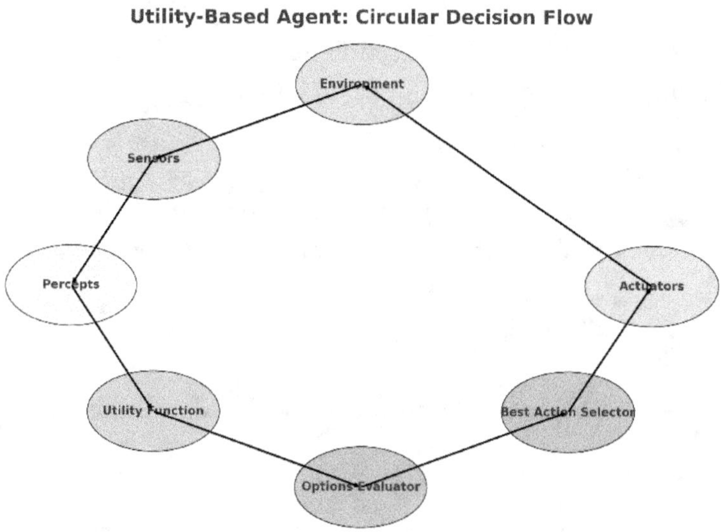

The diagram above illustrates the workflow of a utility-based agent. This structure enables the agent to operate with nuance and flexibility, especially in environments with competing priorities, uncertainty, or trade-offs.

🔧 What Is Utility in AI?

Utility represents a numeric value indicating how preferable or valuable an outcome is to the agent. Utility functions allow the agent to:

- Compare complex outcomes
- Reason under uncertainty
- Make decisions that balance conflicting needs (e.g., speed vs. safety)

🔄 How Utility-Based Agents Work

1. Environment

This is the external world the agent interacts with. It includes everything that can be sensed or acted upon.

2. Sensors

The agent uses sensors to gather percepts (data) from the environment, such as location, temperature, object positions, or user input.

3. Percepts

Structured observations that feed into the decision-making process.

4. Utility Function

This core component assigns a numeric score to possible outcomes. For instance:

- In autonomous driving: Safe route = 0.9, Fast route = 0.7, Risky route = 0.2
- In a trading bot: High profit, low risk = 1.0; high profit, high risk = 0.5

Utility is often computed using domain-specific heuristics, expert input, or learned from data.

5. Options Evaluator

Generates a list of possible actions and evaluates their predicted outcomes based on the utility function.

6. Best Action Selector

Chooses the action with the highest utility score. This decision balances trade-offs, handles ambiguity, and allows for adaptive behavior.

7. Actuators

These components carry out the selected action in the environment—like a motor turning, a software call executing, or a message being sent.

Simple Python Example

```
def utility_function(state):
    # Higher score is better
    return {
        "safe_path": 0.9,
        "fast_path": 0.7,
        "risky_path": 0.2
    }[state]


def decide_action(percepts):
    options = ["safe_path", "fast_path", "risky_path"]
    scored = [(opt, utility_function(opt)) for opt in options]
    return max(scored, key=lambda x: x[1])[0]
# Example usage
action = decide_action(percepts=None)
print("Selected action:", action)
```

✅ Advantages of Utility-Based Agents

- **Fine-grained decisions**: Doesn't just meet goals—it chooses the *best* among many.

- **Handles uncertainty**: Can integrate probability with expected utility.
- **Customizable**: Easily adapts to different objectives via the utility function.

❌ **Challenges**

- **Complex utility design**: Defining meaningful utility functions can be hard.
- **Computation-heavy**: May require evaluating many scenarios per decision.
- **Requires accurate models**: Garbage-in, garbage-out applies to utility too.

Summary

Component	Purpose
Environment	External system the agent operates in
Sensors	Collect data from the environment
Percepts	Processed observations
Utility Function	Scores outcomes numerically
Options Evaluator	Predicts and scores possible actions
Best Action Selector	Picks the highest-utility option
Actuators	Execute chosen action

Utility-based systems are a foundational tool in AI applications where **flexible, informed choices** matter: autonomous driving, recommendation engines, smart assistants, and more. By assigning values to outcomes and reasoning with those values, agents become more human-like in how they prioritize and choose their actions.

Hands-on Example: Basic Agent Navigation System

Navigation is one of the most foundational capabilities in autonomous agents. Whether you're designing a delivery robot, a virtual game character, or a drone, the ability to move from point A to point B intelligently is critical. This hands-on example shows how to build a basic **agent navigation system** with clear, modular components.

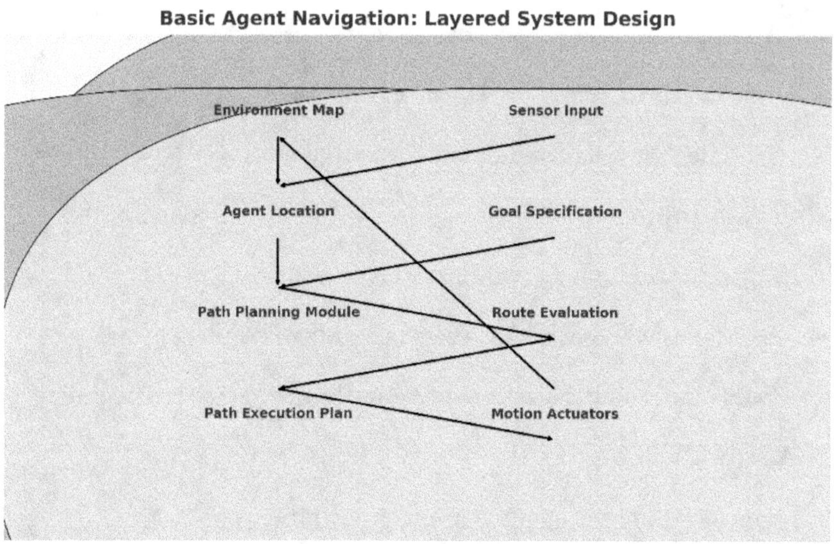

The diagram above illustrates the core functional blocks involved in agent navigation. Each component serves a specific role in sensing, planning, evaluating, and executing movement.

🧭 Overview of the Navigation Flow

A navigation system is typically a **goal-based, model-aware** agent architecture. The agent maintains awareness of:

- Where it is
- Where it needs to go
- What obstacles or rules exist
- The best way to reach its goal

⚙ Component Breakdown

1. Environment Map

- A spatial representation of the agent's surroundings.
- Can be a grid, graph, or 3D structure.
- Provides the data foundation for path planning.

2. Sensor Input

- Captures the agent's real-time perceptions.
- Examples: GPS, LIDAR, camera, simulated grid sensors.
- Feeds into the localization and environmental understanding.

3. Agent Location

- Tracks where the agent is in the environment.
- May include orientation and velocity.
- Critical for starting and updating the plan dynamically.

4. Goal Specification

- Defines the agent's destination.

- Can be static (fixed point) or dynamic (user-driven or context-sensitive).

5. Path Planning Module

- Generates one or more routes from the current location to the goal.
- Algorithms: A*, Dijkstra, RRT, or graph-based search.
- Considers map structure, movement rules, and constraints.

6. Route Evaluation

- Scores alternative routes using utility metrics like:
  - Path length
  - Safety (obstacle clearance)
  - Energy efficiency
  - Time cost
- Helps choose the most appropriate path, not just the shortest.

7. Path Execution Plan

- Converts the selected route into a sequence of movement commands or waypoints.

8. Motion Actuators

- The agent's output interface for movement.
- In a robot, these could be wheels or rotors.
- In software, this could mean issuing commands in a simulation.

🛠 Sample Navigation Loop in Python

```
class NavigationAgent:
    def __init__(self, environment, start, goal):
        self.map = environment
        self.position = start
        self.goal = goal

    def sense(self):
        return self.map.get_obstacles_near(self.position)

    def plan(self):
        return self.a_star(self.position, self.goal)

    def evaluate(self, path):
        return len(path)  # simplistic utility = shorter is better

    def act(self, path):
        for step in path:
            self.position = step
            print("Moved to:", step)

    def a_star(self, start, goal):
```

```
        # Placeholder logic
        return [start, goal]


# Initialize
env = ... # your environment object
agent = NavigationAgent(env, (0, 0), (4, 4))


# Run
obstacles = agent.sense()
path = agent.plan()
score = agent.evaluate(path)
agent.act(path)
```

✅ **Why This Design Works**

- **Modularity**: Each part of the system can be upgraded independently.
- **Flexibility**: Works for both real-world and simulated environments.
- **Scalability**: Can be expanded with real-time replanning, SLAM, or multi-agent routing.

Summary Table

Component	Role
Environment Map	Defines the spatial constraints and terrain
Sensor Input	Captures real-time data from surroundings
Agent Location	Tracks agent's current position
Goal Specification	Defines the navigation objective
Path Planning Module	Finds possible paths to the goal
Route Evaluation	Ranks and selects the best available route
Path Execution Plan	Converts path into actionable steps
Motion Actuators	Executes movements and updates the environment

This structure is a baseline for building increasingly complex agents. Later versions can include dynamic map updates, probabilistic path prediction, multi-agent coordination, and reinforcement learning for adaptive motion.

Part 3: Professional Development and Advanced Techniques
Chapter 7: Machine Learning for AI Agents

Supervised, Unsupervised, and Reinforcement Learning

Machine learning (ML) empowers AI agents to improve their behavior based on data, feedback, and experiences. There are three foundational paradigms in ML that influence how AI agents are trained: **supervised learning**, **unsupervised learning**, and **reinforcement learning**. Each approach supports different types of tasks and environments.

Machine Learning Approaches for AI Agents

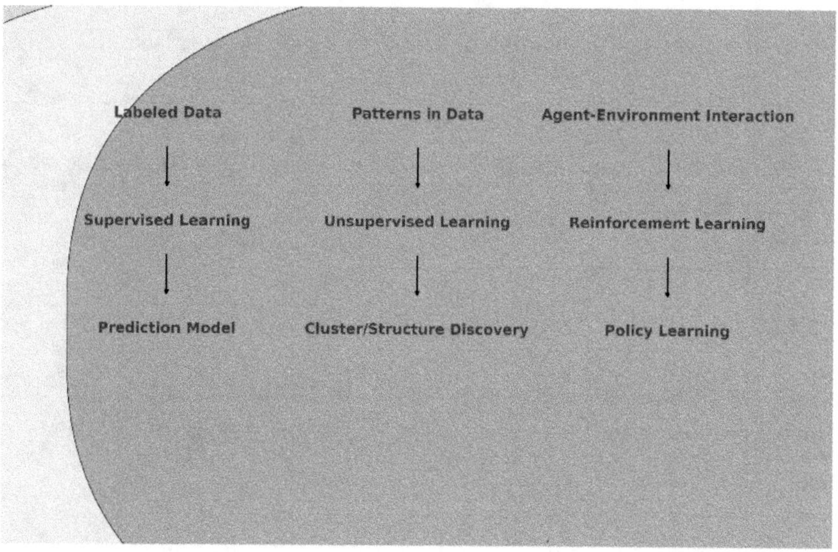

The diagram above illustrates the flow of each paradigm, from the type of data they require to the kind of learning they perform and the outcomes they produce.

🧠 1. Supervised Learning

What It Is:

Supervised learning teaches an agent using **labeled data**—pairs of inputs and correct outputs. The agent learns to map inputs to expected outcomes.

Data:

- Example: Images labeled as "cat" or "dog"
- Used for classification, regression, and structured prediction

Output:

- A model capable of making predictions on new, unseen data

Example Use Case:

- An agent that detects spam emails by training on thousands of labeled examples.

🔍 2. Unsupervised Learning

What It Is:

Unsupervised learning involves **unlabeled data**. The agent tries to uncover hidden patterns, structures, or groupings within the data.

Data:

- Example: Customer purchase histories with no predefined categories

Output:

- Clusters or associations
- Structural insights like dimensionality reduction

Example Use Case:

- An AI agent segments users based on browsing behavior for targeted advertising.

🎮 3. Reinforcement Learning (RL)

What It Is:

Reinforcement learning is based on **trial-and-error interaction with an environment**. The agent receives **rewards or penalties** and learns to maximize long-term reward.

Data:

- No initial labeled data; learning happens through episodes of experience

Output:

- A **policy**: a mapping from states to actions that maximizes expected reward

Example Use Case:

- A game-playing agent that learns to win through repeated play (e.g., AlphaGo, Dota bots).

🤖 How Each Supports AI Agents

Learning Type	Training Data	Agent Behavior Learned	Typical Applications
Supervised Learning	Labeled input-output pairs	Prediction, classification	Perception systems, diagnostics
Unsupervised Learning	Unlabeled data	Pattern discovery, clustering	Market analysis, anomaly detection
Reinforcement Learning	Environment feedback	Goal-directed action strategies	Robotics, games, autonomous systems

Summary

- **Supervised learning** helps agents learn by example.
- **Unsupervised learning** helps agents discover hidden structures.
- **Reinforcement learning** teaches agents to make decisions by acting and learning from consequences.

In practice, many advanced AI systems **combine** these approaches—for instance, using supervised learning to extract features and reinforcement learning to learn behaviors. Mastery of these ML paradigms is essential for anyone building intelligent, adaptive agents.

Deep Reinforcement Learning

Deep reinforcement learning (DRL) combines reinforcement learning with deep neural networks, enabling agents to make decisions in high-dimensional environments. It allows AI agents to learn complex behaviors directly from raw sensory input, such as pixels or sensor arrays, by trial and error.

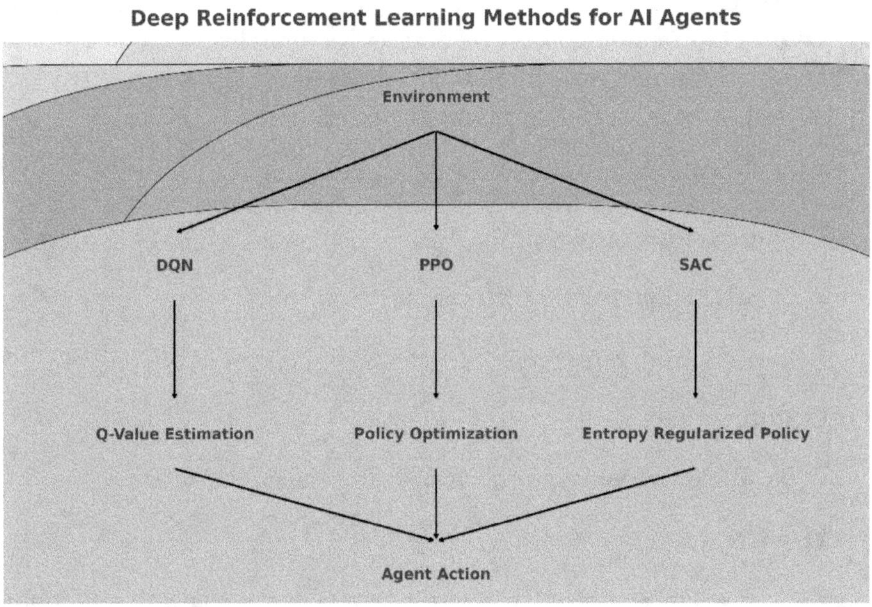

The diagram above illustrates the three major families of DRL methods - **Deep Q-Networks (DQN), Proximal Policy Optimization (PPO)**, and **Soft Actor-Critic (SAC)** - and how they interact with the environment to choose actions.

🔄 Core DRL Loop

In all DRL approaches, the basic loop is:

1. **Observe** the environment state.
2. **Choose** an action.

3. **Receive** a reward and new state.
4. **Update** the policy or value estimate to improve future actions.

What differentiates DQN, PPO, and SAC is how they represent the policy and update it.

📘 DQN: Deep Q-Network

DQN is a value-based method that uses a neural network to approximate the Q-value function, which estimates the expected reward of taking a certain action in a given state.

Characteristics:

- Discrete action spaces
- Uses a target network for stability
- Learns from replay memory (stored past experiences)

Output:

- Chooses the action with the highest predicted Q-value

Use Case:

- Atari games, where the environment is discrete and visual input is used

📘 PPO: Proximal Policy Optimization

PPO is a policy gradient method that directly learns a probability distribution over actions.

Characteristics:

- Uses a clipped objective to prevent large policy updates
- Balances exploration and exploitation
- More stable than traditional policy gradient methods

Output:

- Stochastic policy (samples action based on learned probabilities)

Use Case:

- Robotics, continuous control tasks like walking or manipulation

■ SAC: Soft Actor-Critic

SAC is an off-policy algorithm that combines both value and policy learning and adds **entropy regularization** to encourage exploration.

Characteristics:

- Optimizes for both expected reward and entropy (uncertainty)
- Works in continuous action spaces
- Highly sample-efficient and stable

Output:

- Learns both actor and critic networks
- Selects actions to maximize both value and exploration

Use Case:

- Complex continuous environments like simulation-based reinforcement

✅ Comparison Table

Feature	DQN	PPO	SAC
Type	Value-based	Policy-based	Actor-Critic + Entropy
Action Space	Discrete	Continuous or discrete	Continuous
Stability	Medium	High	Very High
Sample Efficiency	Low	Medium	High
Exploration Strategy	ε-greedy	Implicit (stochastic policy)	Explicit (entropy bonus)
Ideal Use Case	Game playing (discrete)	Robotics, tasks with noise	High-performance continuous

🧠 Final Takeaway

These three deep reinforcement learning methods form the core of most modern AI agent training systems:

- Use **DQN** when your environment is **simple and discrete**.
- Use **PPO** when you need **reliable policy optimization**.
- Use **SAC** when facing **complex, continuous environments** where exploration is critical.

Mastering these algorithms enables you to build agents that can learn strategies, adapt to dynamic environments, and improve autonomously over time.

Implementing Learning-Based Agents from Scratch

Building a learning-based agent from the ground up is one of the most rewarding and technically rich exercises in AI. These agents adapt to their environment over time using data, experience, and feedback.

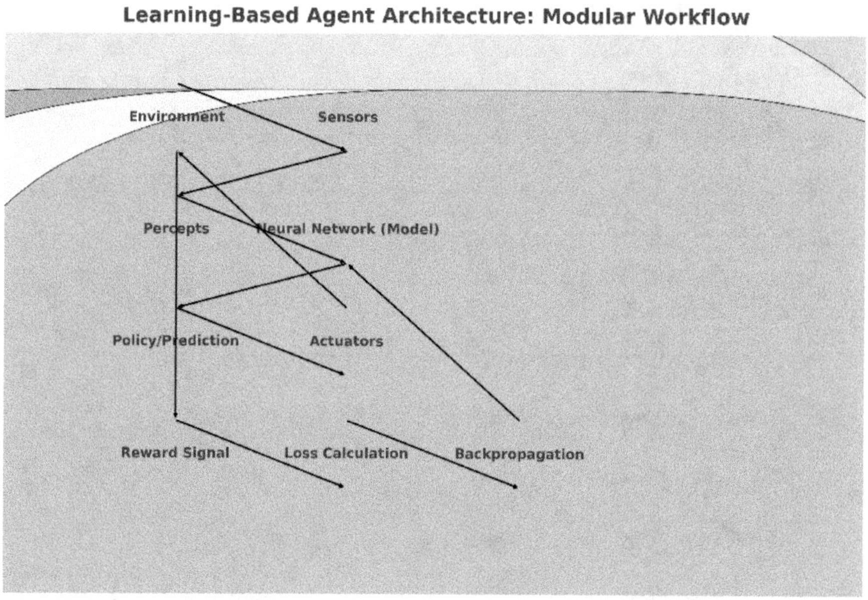

The chart above outlines the system architecture of a basic **learning-based AI agent**, showing how inputs, decisions, and learning components are connected in a loop.

🧠 What is a Learning-Based Agent?

A learning-based agent uses machine learning - typically with a neural network - to predict actions or policies based on sensory input. It improves its behavior using **feedback** in the form of rewards, losses, or performance metrics.

Component Breakdown

1. Environment

- The external world or simulation the agent interacts with.
- It provides observable data (via sensors) and rewards based on the agent's actions.

2. Sensors

- Capture data from the environment (e.g., images, distance, velocity).
- Deliver this information as raw inputs.

3. Percepts

- Structured, preprocessed versions of the sensor data.
- These form the actual input to the neural network.

4. Neural Network (Model)

- The agent's internal "brain".
- Maps percepts to decisions (actions or value predictions).
- This model gets updated through training using feedback.

5. Policy/Prediction

- The output of the model—what action to take, or how good a state is.
- Can be deterministic (fixed action) or stochastic (sampled from probabilities).

6. Actuators

- The effectors that carry out the agent's decision.
- Could be motors, commands, API calls, or simulated actions.

7. Reward Signal

- Comes from the environment after an action is taken.
- Indicates success, failure, or degree of performance.
- Drives learning by telling the agent how well it's doing.

8. Loss Calculation

- Computes the error between the expected and actual outcome.
- Could be based on predicted reward vs. actual reward, or target policy.

9. Backpropagation

- Standard deep learning technique for adjusting model weights.
- Minimizes loss by updating the neural network using gradient descent.

Learning Loop Summary

1. The agent observes the environment through **sensors**.
2. It forms **percepts** and feeds them to a **neural network**.
3. The model produces an action (**policy/prediction**).
4. **Actuators** apply the action to the **environment**.
5. The environment gives a **reward**, which is used to compute **loss**.
6. The model is updated via **backpropagation** based on the error.

This loop repeats, with the agent refining its behavior continuously.

Example: Python Pseudo-Code

```
class LearningAgent:
    def __init__(self, model):
```

```
        self.model = model  # a neural network
        self.optimizer = torch.optim.Adam(model.parameters())

    def act(self, percept):
        return self.model(percept).argmax()

    def learn(self, percept, action, reward, next_percept):
        prediction = self.model(percept)[action]
        target = reward + max(self.model(next_percept).detach())
        loss = (prediction - target) ** 2

        self.optimizer.zero_grad()
        loss.backward()
        self.optimizer.step()
```

✅ Benefits of Learning-Based Agents

- **Adaptivity**: Can improve with experience without manual rules.
- **Scalability**: Works across environments with minimal structural change.
- **Intelligence**: Enables behaviors that aren't explicitly programmed.

❌ Challenges

- Requires significant training data or experience.
- Sensitive to hyperparameters and reward structure.

- May be unstable or sample-inefficient without good architecture.

Summary Table

Component	**Role**
Environment	Provides inputs and evaluates performance
Sensors & Percepts	Capture and format information for the agent
Neural Network	Learns a mapping from input to action/value
Policy/Prediction	Selects an action to take
Actuators	Execute the decision
Reward Signal	Feedback from the environment
Loss Calculation	Determines the error in behavior
Backpropagation	Adjusts model to reduce future errors

This foundational agent design can be extended to implement **supervised**, **reinforcement**, or **unsupervised learning** strategies, depending on the task. Once understood, it opens the door to developing agents for games, robotics, finance, autonomous vehicles, and more.

Chapter 8: Multi-Agent Systems

Fundamentals of Multi-Agent Environments

As AI systems evolve, many real-world applications demand not just one intelligent agent, but multiple agents working **together**, **independently**, or even **competitively** within a shared environment. These are called **Multi-Agent Systems (MAS)**.

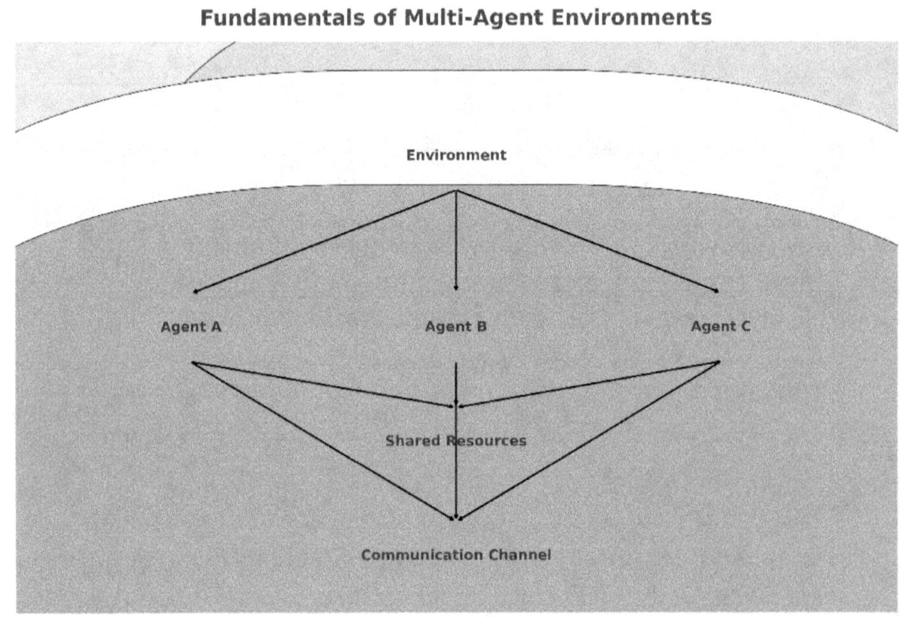

The diagram above illustrates the core structure of a multi-agent environment, featuring multiple agents (A, B, C) interacting with a shared environment, resources, and communication channel.

What is a Multi-Agent System?

A **Multi-Agent System** is a collection of intelligent agents that operate in a shared space. Each agent:

- Perceives the environment

- Acts upon it
- May interact with other agents
- Has individual goals, capabilities, and knowledge

Agents can be **cooperative**, **competitive**, or **mixed** in their behavior.

🔄 Core Components of Multi-Agent Environments

1. Environment

- The space where agents operate
- Provides sensory data and responds to actions
- Could be physical (e.g., robotics arena) or digital (e.g., simulation)

2. Agents

Each agent can:

- Make autonomous decisions
- Learn or adapt over time
- Collaborate or compete with others

In the diagram:

- **Agent A**, **Agent B**, and **Agent C** each act independently but within the same space.

3. Shared Resources

- Entities or assets accessed by multiple agents (e.g., time slots, bandwidth, space, power)
- May lead to **conflicts**, requiring coordination or negotiation

4. Communication Channel

- Enables agents to share information
- Critical for **coordination, planning**, or **teamwork**
- Communication may be direct (messages) or indirect (through environment signals)

🤖 Types of Agent Interactions

Type	Description	Example Scenario
Cooperative	Agents work together to achieve a common goal	Swarm robots building a structure
Competitive	Agents compete for limited resources	Bidding in a distributed market
Mixed	Agents cooperate in some aspects, compete in others	Multiplayer strategy games

🛠 Characteristics of Multi-Agent Environments

- **Decentralization**: No single agent controls the entire system.
- **Local perception**: Agents have partial views of the world.
- **Autonomy**: Each agent makes its own decisions.
- **Scalability**: New agents can be added or removed with minimal redesign.

✅ Benefits

- **Scalability**: Divide complex problems among specialized agents.
- **Robustness**: Failure of one agent doesn't crash the system.

- **Flexibility**: Can handle dynamic environments and evolving goals.

❌ Challenges

- **Coordination complexity**: More agents = more potential conflicts.
- **Communication overhead**: Can become a bottleneck.
- **Non-stationarity**: Each agent's learning may affect others, making the environment unstable.

Summary Table

Component	Role
Environment	Provides the shared space and rules of interaction
Agents (A, B, C)	Perceive, decide, and act autonomously
Shared Resources	Entities accessed by multiple agents
Communication Channel	Facilitates coordination and strategy sharing

Multi-agent systems are foundational in applications like smart cities, autonomous vehicles, robotics teams, economic simulations, and multi-player games. Understanding the dynamics of such environments is key to building robust, scalable, and intelligent systems that mirror the complexity of the real world.

Coordination, Collaboration, and Competition Strategies

In multi-agent systems (MAS), agents often operate in shared environments with overlapping or opposing goals. Designing how they **coordinate**, **collaborate**, or **compete** is central to system efficiency and agent success. The chart above visualizes these strategies, breaking down each into core mechanisms and interactions.

🤝 Coordination

Coordination is the process of managing dependencies and avoiding conflicts between agents. Agents don't necessarily share goals, but they need to synchronize actions to avoid interference.

Key Mechanisms:

- **Shared Goals**: Agents align on common outcomes (e.g., assembling parts in a factory).
- **Task Allocation**: Divides complex tasks into subtasks distributed among agents (e.g., in swarm robotics or logistics).

Examples:

- Traffic signals coordinating autonomous vehicles.
- Multi-robot systems scheduling delivery without overlap.

Collaboration

Collaboration goes a step further than coordination: agents actively work together to achieve a shared objective, often combining their capabilities.

Key Mechanisms:

- **Information Sharing**: Agents share local observations or intentions to build a collective view of the world.
- **Joint Planning**: Agents co-develop strategies, combining resources or synchronizing timelines.

Examples:

- Rescue robots planning a building sweep together.
- Teams of drones mapping terrain in parallel.

Competition

Competition arises when agents have conflicting goals or limited resources. Competitive strategies focus on maximizing individual success while minimizing rivals' performance.

Key Mechanisms:

- **Limited Resources**: Agents compete for bandwidth, space, energy, or task priority.
- **Strategic Behavior**: Agents use prediction, deception, or bidding to outmaneuver others.

Examples:

- Bidding in distributed auctions.
- Game AI fighting for territory or rewards.

Strategy Interactions

Multi-agent systems often involve a mix of all three strategies. For example:

- Autonomous vehicles coordinate lane merging.
- They collaborate with nearby cars using shared intent.
- They compete with others for space or speed.

✅ Benefits of Strategy Design

Strategy	Benefits	Challenges
Coordination	Reduces conflict and redundancy	Requires synchronization protocols
Collaboration	Increases system performance	Needs trust, communication, and alignment
Competition	Encourages innovation and efficiency	Risk of conflict and inefficiency

Summary Table

Concept	Function	Common Techniques
Coordination	Syncing tasks among agents	Shared protocols, task scheduling
Collaboration	Working jointly toward a shared goal	Communication, joint planning, team models
Competition	Maximizing individual gains	Game theory, auctions, reinforcement learning

Mastering these strategies allows you to build intelligent systems that reflect the dynamics of the real world, from **market simulations** to **cooperative robotics** to **multi-player games**. A successful MAS design balances these forces based on the nature of the task and agent interactions.

Real-World Examples (Autonomous Vehicles, Robotics)

Multi-agent systems are no longer theoretical - they are deeply integrated into real-world applications where multiple intelligent entities must sense, act, and learn in shared spaces.

Coordination, Collaboration, and Competition in Multi-Agent Systems

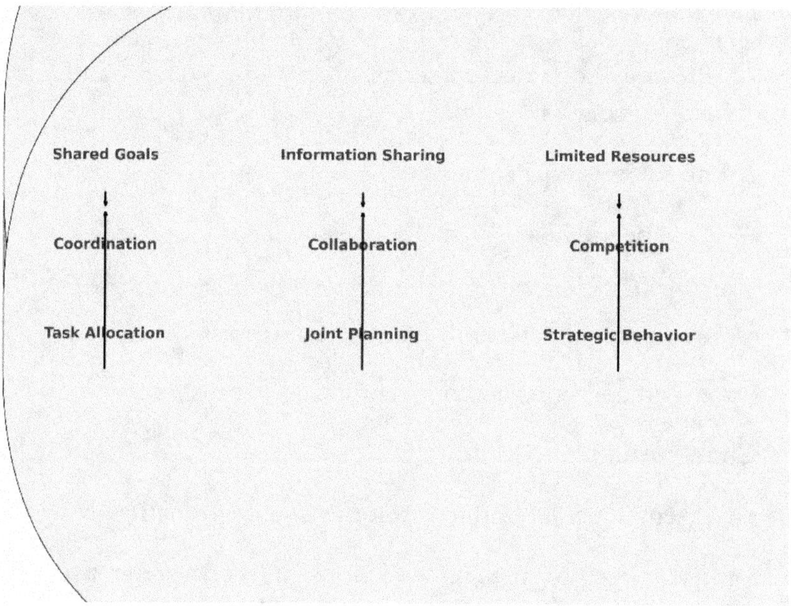

The chart above illustrates two major domains where multi-agent systems thrive: **autonomous vehicles** and **collaborative robotics**.

🚙 Autonomous Vehicles

In modern traffic systems, **self-driving cars** act as autonomous agents in a dynamic multi-agent environment. Each vehicle makes real-time decisions while being aware of others around it.

Key Applications:

1. Traffic Flow Coordination

- Vehicles use V2V (vehicle-to-vehicle) and V2I (vehicle-to-infrastructure) communication.
- Share data like speed, position, and intentions.
- Prevents bottlenecks, reduces stop-and-go traffic, and improves overall flow.

2. Lane Merging Protocols

- Cars negotiate entry into congested lanes (e.g., freeway on-ramps).
- Use decentralized coordination and priority rules.
- Avoid collisions without centralized control.

Characteristics:

- Agents operate both cooperatively and competitively.
- Local decision-making with global traffic awareness.
- Integrates planning, perception, and negotiation.

🤖 Collaborative Robotics

In industrial and emergency environments, multiple robots work together or alongside humans, each playing a specific role.

Key Applications:

1. Warehouse Automation

- Robots handle picking, packing, and delivery inside fulfillment centers.

- Coordinate to avoid collisions, optimize paths, and share battery stations.
- Real-time path planning and task allocation are essential.

2. Rescue Operations

- Swarms of drones or ground robots search collapsed buildings or disaster zones.
- Share maps, split search zones, and collaborate on object detection.
- Can function with minimal or no communication infrastructure.

Characteristics:

- High reliance on coordination and task distribution.
- Often requires robust fault tolerance and autonomy.
- Dynamic environments with real-time adaptation.

Shared Principles in Real-World Multi-Agent Systems

Feature	Description
Decentralized Control	Each agent operates independently
Local Perception	Agents have partial knowledge and must infer the rest
Real-Time Constraints	Fast decision-making is critical
Communication & Negotiation	Optional but enhances performance and coordination
Mixed Interactions	Can be cooperative, competitive, or both

✅ Benefits of Using MAS in These Domains

- **Efficiency**: Optimizes tasks like routing and area coverage.
- **Scalability**: Systems can expand by adding more agents.
- **Robustness**: Failure of one agent doesn't compromise the entire system.
- **Adaptivity**: Agents adjust to changes in the environment or other agents.

The use of multi-agent systems in real-world domains like autonomous vehicles and robotics is transforming how intelligent systems are built. They reflect **real human-like dynamics**—negotiating, cooperating, and learning from others. By understanding these implementations, developers can build agents that thrive in shared, dynamic environments.

Chapter 9: Natural Language Processing in AI Agents

Chatbots and Conversational Agents

As human-computer interaction evolves, AI agents that can understand and generate language - known as **chatbots** or **conversational agents** - are becoming central to user experience. These systems are powered by **Natural Language Processing (NLP)**, a branch of AI focused on understanding, interpreting, and responding to human language.

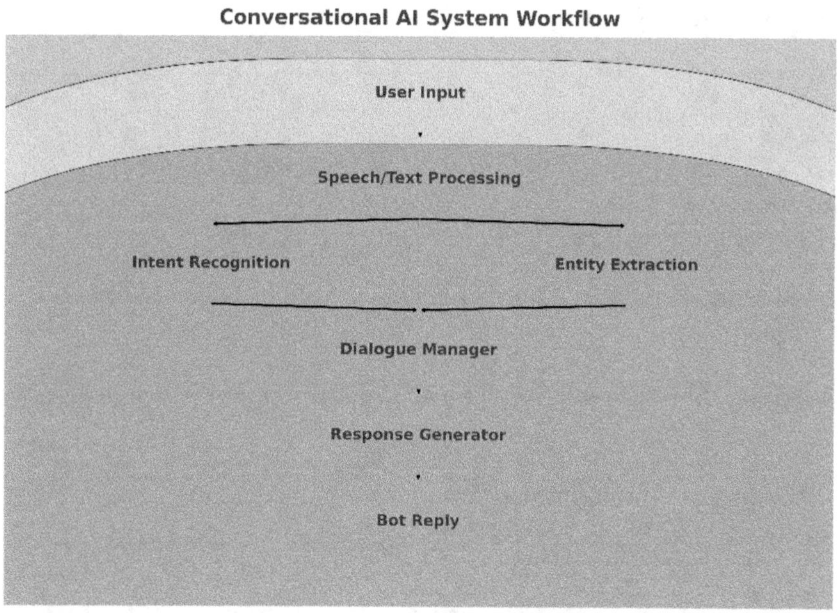

The diagram above outlines the key components of a typical conversational agent, from user input to intelligent response.

Components of a Conversational Agent

1. User Input

- The user initiates interaction via speech or text.

- Examples: "What's the weather today?", "Book me a flight."

2. Speech/Text Processing

- Converts audio to text (speech recognition) or preprocesses written text (tokenization, cleaning).
- May involve:
  - Normalization (e.g., "what's" → "what is")
  - Removing noise like emojis or slang

3. Intent Recognition

- Uses NLP models (often classifiers or transformers) to determine what the user wants.
- Example intents: "BookFlight", "CheckWeather", "PlayMusic"

4. Entity Extraction

- Identifies **named entities** and **keywords** like dates, names, locations.
- Example: "Book a flight to Paris on Monday" → {destination: "Paris", date: "Monday"}

5. Dialogue Manager

- Coordinates the flow of conversation.
- Tracks context (e.g., has the user already given the date?), manages dialogue state.
- Decides next action: ask follow-up, query API, or give response.

6. Response Generator

- Produces the agent's reply.

- Could be rule-based (templated), retrieval-based (select best from a set), or generative (using models like GPT).

7. Bot Reply

- Returns the generated message to the user, via text or speech synthesis.
- Examples: "Your flight to Paris is booked.", "Today's weather is sunny with a high of 22°C."

🤖 Chatbot Types

Type	Description	Examples
Rule-Based	Uses if-else logic and decision trees	Menu-based customer support bots
Retrieval-Based	Selects best response from a dataset	FAQ bots, tech support agents
Generative (Neural)	Uses models to generate novel responses	AI companions, virtual assistants

🔍 Key NLP Techniques Used

Technique	Purpose
Tokenization	Breaks input into words or phrases
Named Entity Recognition (NER)	Finds structured info like dates, names
Intent Classification	Categorizes user input
Context Management	Tracks conversation history
Text Generation	Creates natural language responses

✅ Benefits of Conversational Agents

- **Accessibility**: Users can interact using natural language
- **Scalability**: One agent can handle many users simultaneously
- **Personalization**: Agents can remember user preferences or history

❌ Challenges

- **Ambiguity**: Human language is often vague or context-dependent
- **Context Retention**: Maintaining memory across long conversations
- **Multimodality**: Integrating text, speech, and visual input
- **Bias & Safety**: Ensuring inclusive, non-toxic, fact-based responses

Summary Table

Component	Role
Speech/Text Processing	Converts input into structured data
Intent Recognition	Understands what the user wants
Entity Extraction	Gathers key details from the request
Dialogue Manager	Maintains flow and context
Response Generator	Produces a relevant, natural reply

By understanding the architecture and strategies of conversational systems, developers can build smarter, more human-like agents that serve users effectively - whether in customer service, education, healthcare, or entertainment.

Implementing NLP in Agent Interactions

Implementing NLP in agent interactions goes far beyond simple keyword matching. Modern AI agents must understand user intent, manage conversation flow, and generate human-like responses - all in real time.

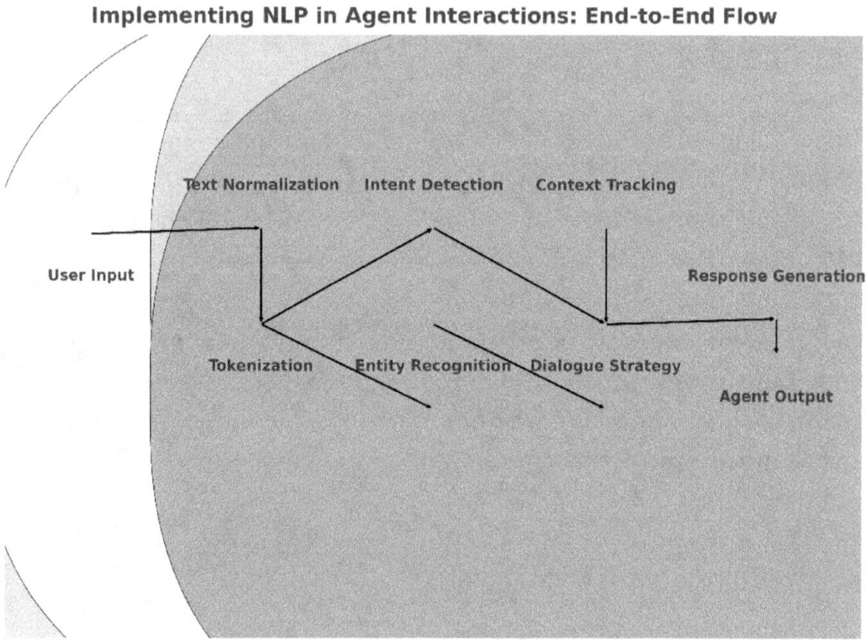

The diagram above represents an end-to-end architecture for NLP-driven agent communication, highlighting each core module in the interaction pipeline.

Step-by-Step NLP Integration Workflow

1. User Input

- The entry point of the interaction, either spoken or typed.
- Must handle variability in language, phrasing, slang, and ambiguity.

2. Text Normalization

- Converts raw input into a consistent, clean format.
- Handles:
  - Contractions (e.g., "don't" → "do not")
  - Casing
  - Spelling corrections
  - Removal of irrelevant symbols

3. Tokenization

- Breaks normalized text into smaller units (tokens) like words or subwords.
- Prepares the input for downstream tasks like classification or tagging.

4. Intent Detection

- Uses machine learning or deep learning to classify the user's goal.
- Common methods:
  - Logistic regression
  - RNNs, CNNs
  - Transformers (e.g., BERT, RoBERTa)

Example Intents:

- BookFlight
- CheckWeather
- OrderFood

5. Entity Recognition

- Extracts key details from user input (e.g., destination, time, product name).
- Can be rule-based or model-driven (NER using CRF or transformer-based models).

6. Context Tracking

- Maintains conversation state over multiple exchanges.
- Enables continuity by remembering prior inputs (e.g., "Book a flight" → "To New York" → "Tomorrow").

7. Dialogue Strategy

- Decides what the agent should do next.
- Strategies include:
  - Ask for clarification
  - Confirm details
  - Provide answer
  - Transition topic

Uses a combination of:

- Dialogue rules
- Policy learning (in advanced setups using RL)
- Memory/context lookups

8. Response Generation

- Produces the actual reply to the user.
- Three main approaches:

  - Rule-based (static templates)
  - Retrieval-based (from a response database)
  - Generative (using models like GPT)

9. Agent Output

- Sends the response back as text or synthesized speech.
- Can also include UI actions, such as opening a booking screen or showing weather data.

✅ Benefits of Modular NLP Integration

Module	Function	Benefit
Normalization	Cleans noisy input	Improves understanding consistency
Tokenization	Structures text	Enables efficient NLP processing
Intent Detection	Understands user goals	Powers intelligent decision-making
Entity Recognition	Extracts context	Enables actionable responses
Dialogue Strategy	Manages flow	Keeps conversation coherent
Response Generation	Crafts replies	Makes the bot feel human-like

By implementing this structured NLP pipeline, AI agents become conversationally aware, responsive, and contextually intelligent.

Whether deployed as chatbots, virtual assistants, or embedded dialogue systems in apps and smart devices, these agents form the backbone of modern natural language interfaces.

Mastering these components unlocks the ability to create scalable, domain-specific, multilingual, and user-friendly AI experiences.

Case Studies

Natural Language Processing (NLP) has become a cornerstone in building intelligent agents that interact with users through conversation. Among the most impactful real-world implementations are **Customer Service Bots** and **Virtual Assistants**.

NLP Use Cases in AI Agents: Customer Support and Virtual Assistant Systems

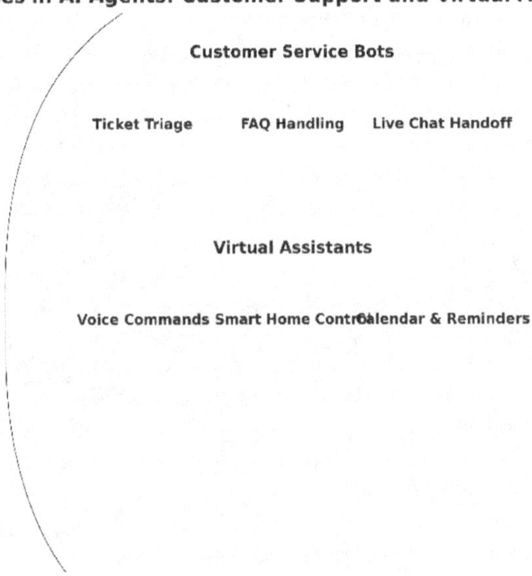

The chart above illustrates these categories and highlights core functions where NLP transforms how these systems operate.

🧑‍💼 Case Study 1: Customer Service Bots

Customer service bots are often the first line of interaction between users and a company. These bots are trained using real customer data and domain-specific intents, enabling them to handle a wide range of service tasks efficiently.

Key NLP-Driven Functions:

1. Ticket Triage

- Automatically classifies and routes incoming support requests.
- Uses intent classification and entity extraction to determine urgency, department, and category.
- Reduces manual sorting and improves response time.

2. FAQ Handling

- Answers commonly asked questions using information retrieval or retrieval-based NLP.
- Employs embeddings or semantic search to match varied user phrasing to stored answers.
- Enhances self-service and reduces call center load.

3. Live Chat Handoff

- Detects when an issue is too complex for the bot and transfers the conversation to a human agent.
- Maintains context for seamless handoff.
- Improves customer satisfaction and avoids dead-ends.

Benefits:

- Operates 24/7
- Reduces operational costs
- Improves consistency in responses

🗣 Case Study 2: Virtual Assistants

Virtual assistants are designed for multi-purpose interaction—helping users manage tasks, answer questions, or control connected devices. They leverage powerful NLP pipelines and context management systems.

Key NLP-Driven Functions:

1. Voice Commands

- Integrates automatic speech recognition (ASR) with NLP to interpret commands like "Set an alarm for 7 AM."
- Requires accurate parsing of commands into intent + parameters.
- Often uses a hybrid approach: voice → text → intent.

2. Smart Home Control

- Maps natural language to device-specific actions (e.g., "Turn on the kitchen lights").
- Handles device disambiguation and contextual cues.
- Can manage multi-turn conversations to refine the command.

3. Calendar & Reminders

- Parses dates, times, and recurrence from casual text (e.g., "Remind me to call Alex tomorrow at noon").
- Uses named entity recognition and date parsers.
- Integrates with scheduling APIs.

✅ Benefits:

- Makes complex tasks simple and natural
- Enhances accessibility

- Continuously improves via user interaction logs

🎯 NLP Techniques at Work

Use Case	NLP Methods Applied
Ticket Triage	Intent classification, entity tagging
FAQ Matching	Semantic similarity, embedding search
Voice Command	ASR, syntactic parsing, action mapping
Smart Device Control	Context resolution, command generation
Calendar Parsing	Temporal entity recognition, slot filling

Summary Table

Application Area	Example Functions	Core Value
Customer Service Bots	Triage, FAQ, Live Handoff	Fast support, high availability
Virtual Assistants	Voice, Smart Control, Reminders	Natural interaction, productivity

By embedding NLP into these systems, developers enable AI agents to understand and respond to user needs with precision and context. These use cases demonstrate how conversational intelligence is no longer experimental - it's an essential part of modern digital interfaces.

Part 4: Deployment and Practical Applications
Chapter 10: Deployment Strategies for AI Agents

Containerization and Docker

Efficient deployment is critical for getting AI agents from development into production. Containerization - particularly using **Docker** - has become the standard for packaging, distributing, and running AI systems reliably across environments.

Docker-Based Deployment Workflow for AI Agents

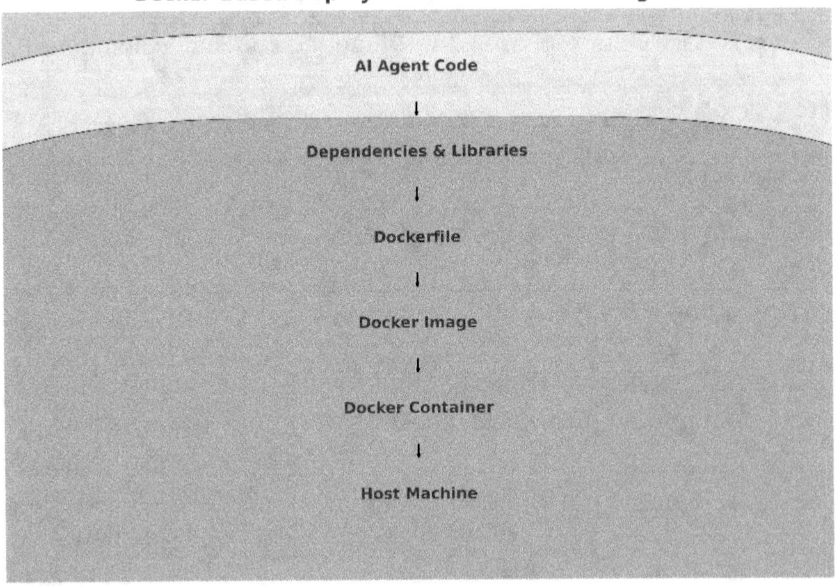

The diagram above shows a step-by-step visual of how AI agents are packaged and deployed using Docker.

🧱 What Is Containerization?

Containerization means packaging the application code along with its runtime environment, libraries, and dependencies into a single, portable unit called a **container**. This ensures that your AI agent runs exactly the same way on any system, regardless of underlying OS differences.

Key Components in Docker Deployment

1. AI Agent Code

- The core logic of your intelligent system.
- Includes models, scripts, utilities, and configuration files.

2. Dependencies & Libraries

- Frameworks like TensorFlow, PyTorch, scikit-learn, Flask, etc.
- Other software your agent needs to function properly (e.g., numpy, transformers, OpenCV).

3. Dockerfile

- A configuration script that defines how the image is built.
- It specifies:
  - Base image (e.g., Python 3.10)
  - Installation of dependencies
  - Copying of source code
  - Start commands (e.g., CMD ["python", "agent.py"])

4. Docker Image

- A snapshot of everything your AI agent needs to run.
- Immutable and reusable.
- Can be stored and shared via Docker Hub or private registries.

5. Docker Container

- A live instance of the Docker image.

- Runs your AI agent in a sandboxed environment.
- Multiple containers can run independently, even on the same host.

6. Host Machine

- The physical or virtual server that runs your containers.
- Can be a laptop, cloud VM, or Kubernetes node.

Deployment Workflow

1. **Develop your AI agent** using Python and your ML framework of choice.
2. **Write a Dockerfile** that defines the environment and execution steps.
3. **Build a Docker image** using the Docker CLI (docker build -t agent-name .).
4. **Run containers** from this image on any target system.
5. Optionally, **push images to a container registry** for distribution and scaling.

✅ Benefits of Docker in AI Deployment

Advantage	Description
Portability	Runs the same way across all environments
Reproducibility	Ensures consistent performance, eliminating "works on my machine" issues
Scalability	Easily deploy multiple agents across servers or cloud instances
Isolation	Prevents dependency clashes between different AI projects
CI/CD Integration	Simplifies automation and version control in deployment pipelines

🛠 Example Dockerfile for a Python AI Agent

```
FROM python:3.10-slim

WORKDIR /app

COPY requirements.txt .

RUN pip install -r requirements.txt

COPY . .

CMD ["python", "agent.py"]
```

📦 Best Practices

- Use minimal base images (e.g., python:3.10-slim) to reduce size.
- Pin dependency versions in requirements.txt.

- Keep containers stateless; use volumes or external services for storage.
- Use Docker Compose or Kubernetes for orchestrating multi-agent systems.

Containerization is the bridge between development and production. For AI agents, where consistency, speed, and scalability matter, Docker offers a robust solution. It lets developers focus on building intelligent behavior while abstracting away the headaches of deployment and system compatibility.

Cloud Deployment

Cloud platforms offer scalable, flexible, and production-grade environments for deploying AI agents. Whether you're deploying a customer-facing chatbot, an inference API, or a reinforcement learning agent, cloud providers like **AWS**, **Azure**, and **Google Cloud Platform (GCP)** offer powerful tools and services tailored for AI workloads.

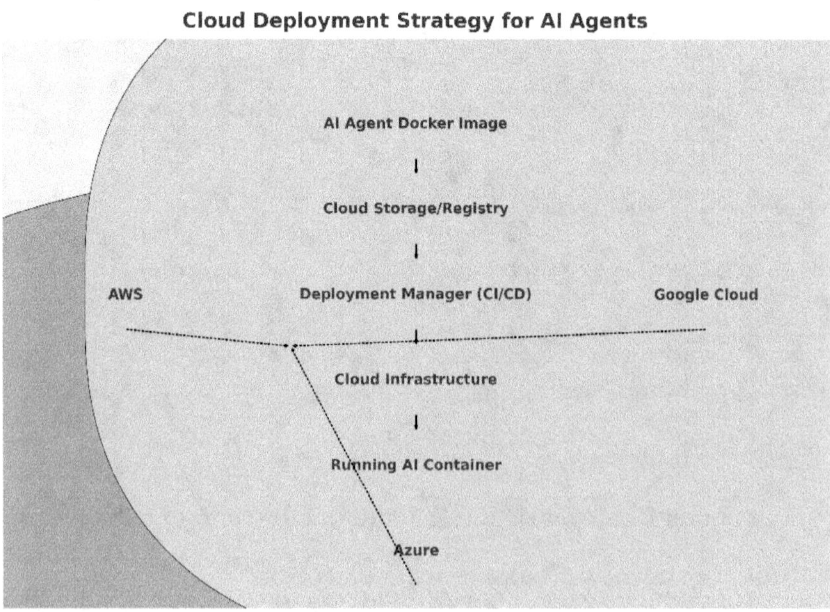

The diagram above outlines a typical cloud deployment flow for containerized AI agents, highlighting how major cloud platforms support deployment and runtime infrastructure.

☁ Cloud Deployment Pipeline Overview

1. AI Agent Docker Image

- The AI agent is packaged in a Docker image that includes all code, dependencies, and runtime.
- Ensures consistency across development and production environments.

2. Cloud Storage or Registry

- The Docker image is uploaded to a container registry like:
    - **Amazon ECR (Elastic Container Registry)**
    - **Azure Container Registry**
    - **Google Container Registry (GCR)**
- This acts as a repository from which cloud services can pull the image for deployment.

3. Deployment Manager / CI-CD

- Tools like **GitHub Actions, GitLab CI**, or cloud-native services (e.g., AWS CodePipeline, Azure DevOps, Google Cloud Build) automate the deployment process.
- Upon code changes or container updates, these systems trigger new deployments.
- Configures resource scaling, networking, and access permissions.

4. Cloud Infrastructure

- The deployed containers run on managed services:

  - **Amazon ECS / EKS / Lambda**
  - **Azure Kubernetes Service (AKS) / App Services**
  - **Google Kubernetes Engine (GKE) / Cloud Run**
- Supports auto-scaling, load balancing, and secure API endpoints.

5. Running AI Container

- The live, running instance of your AI agent.
- Exposes endpoints for inference or conversation (e.g., REST, gRPC, WebSocket).
- May connect to databases, analytics services, or other microservices.

🔍 Platform-Specific Highlights

Platform	Key Services for AI Deployment
AWS	ECS, EKS, Lambda, SageMaker, ECR, CodePipeline
Azure	AKS, Azure ML, App Services, Azure DevOps, Container Registry
Google Cloud	GKE, Cloud Run, AI Platform, Artifact Registry

✅ Benefits of Cloud Deployment

Benefit	Description
Scalability	Automatically scale containers up/down based on load
Reliability	High uptime, monitoring, and disaster recovery
Security	Managed identity, encryption, IAM roles
Speed	Rapid CI/CD pipelines and blue-green deployments
Global Access	Serve users from different regions using CDNs

🧠 **Best Practices**

- Use environment variables for configuration (not hardcoded settings).
- Monitor usage with built-in tools like AWS CloudWatch, Azure Monitor, or GCP Logging.
- Enable auto-scaling for load-balanced deployments.
- Leverage GPU support (e.g., for inference with TensorFlow, PyTorch).
- Secure APIs using API Gateway, OAuth, or IAM policies.

Cloud deployment is the final bridge between building an AI agent and delivering it as a usable product. By leveraging Docker and managed cloud services, you gain the power to scale, monitor, and iterate on your agents quickly and reliably. Whether you're deploying a single bot or orchestrating a fleet of micro-agents, cloud platforms provide the infrastructure to make it seamless.

Edge Deployment Considerations

Deploying AI agents to the edge - on devices such as smartphones, drones, industrial sensors, or smart home hubs - offers fast, offline, and localized intelligence. Unlike cloud-based deployments, **edge deployment** demands tight control over resource usage, latency, and connectivity.

Edge Deployment Workflow for AI Agents

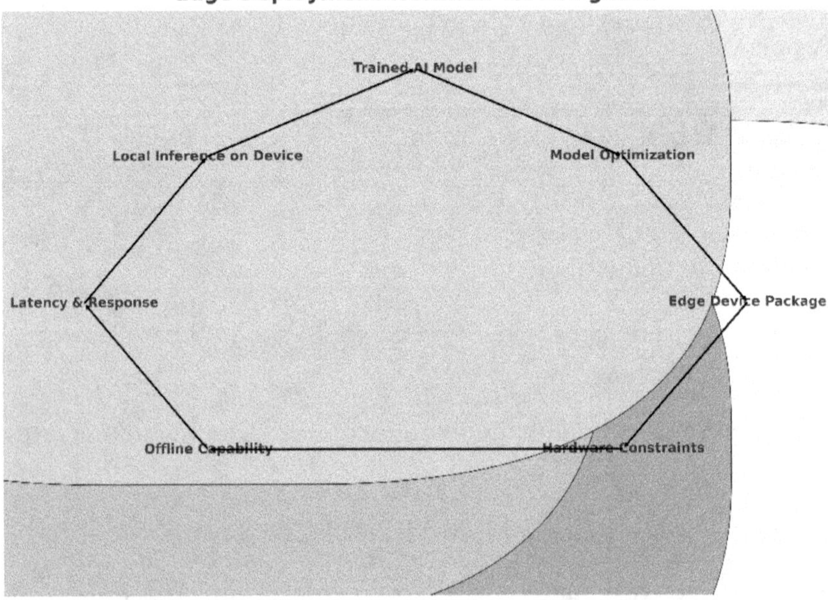

The diagram above outlines the edge deployment workflow for AI agents and highlights the critical factors that influence successful implementation.

🚀 What Is Edge Deployment?

Edge deployment means running AI models directly on end-user devices, without relying on cloud servers. This reduces latency and network dependency while improving real-time performance and data privacy.

Edge Deployment Workflow Breakdown

1. Trained AI Model

- Initially developed and trained on a cloud or local workstation using frameworks like TensorFlow, PyTorch, or ONNX.
- Includes all model weights, architecture, and training logic.

2. Model Optimization (Quantization, Pruning)

- Before deployment, models are optimized to run on low-power, low-memory environments:
    - **Quantization** reduces model precision (e.g., from 32-bit floats to 8-bit integers).
    - **Pruning** removes unnecessary weights or neurons.
    - **Knowledge Distillation** transfers knowledge from a large model to a smaller one.

3. Edge Device Package

- Combines the optimized model, agent logic, and inference engine (e.g., TensorFlow Lite, ONNX Runtime Mobile).
- Packaged for deployment on target hardware (Raspberry Pi, NVIDIA Jetson, Android device, etc.).

4. Hardware Constraints

- Devices often have limited:
    - **CPU/GPU capacity**
    - **RAM/storage**
    - **Battery life**

- The deployment must be efficient to avoid degrading device performance.

5. Latency & Real-Time Response

- In many edge use cases (e.g., object detection in drones), **real-time processing** is essential.
- Running inference locally eliminates round-trip delay to the cloud, enabling instant feedback.

6. Offline Capabilities

- Edge AI agents can operate without internet access.
- Especially useful in:
    - Remote locations (agriculture, exploration)
    - Privacy-sensitive scenarios (health monitoring)
    - Emergency or mission-critical systems

7. Local Inference on Device

- The final AI agent performs predictions directly on the edge device.
- May also store results locally or sync with the cloud periodically.

✅ Benefits of Edge Deployment

Feature	Advantage
Low Latency	Eliminates cloud round-trip delays
Data Privacy	Keeps data local to the device
Offline Operation	Works without an internet connection
Cost Efficiency	Reduces cloud computation and data transfer fees
Real-Time Processing	Critical for time-sensitive applications like robotics

🔍 Use Case Examples

- **Smartphones**: On-device voice assistants, real-time translation, image recognition
- **Drones**: Visual navigation, obstacle avoidance
- **Factories**: Real-time defect detection and sorting
- **Healthcare**: Wearables doing on-device heart rate monitoring or anomaly detection

Summary Table

Stage	Description
Trained AI Model	Initial model developed in a full training pipeline
Model Optimization	Reduces model size and speeds up inference
Edge Device Packaging	Builds deployable unit with model and runtime
Hardware Considerations	Resource-aware deployment strategies
Latency & Offline Capabilities	Enables fast, local, private AI execution

Edge AI deployment is a crucial evolution in making intelligent systems more responsive, robust, and accessible in environments where cloud connectivity is limited or undesirable. Designing for the edge means thinking deeply about optimization, autonomy, and the unique constraints of embedded systems.

Best Practices for Scalable Systems

Deploying scalable AI agent systems isn't just about getting a model into production - it's about ensuring that the system remains fast, flexible, reliable, and maintainable at scale.

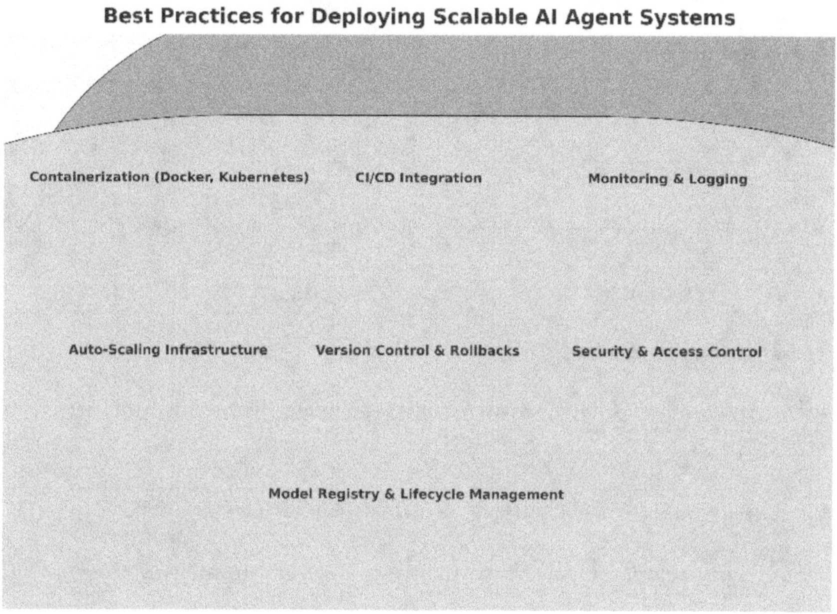

The chart above summarizes key best practices for managing deployment at scale, from infrastructure choices to operational policies.

Best Practices for Scalable AI Deployment

1. Containerization (Docker, Kubernetes)

- Use **Docker** to package your AI agents with all dependencies, ensuring consistent environments across development, testing, and production.
- Use **Kubernetes** or similar orchestrators to deploy, scale, and manage containers.

- Supports high-availability setups and fault tolerance.

2. CI/CD Integration

- Set up **Continuous Integration/Continuous Deployment** pipelines using tools like GitHub Actions, GitLab CI, or Jenkins.
- Automate:
  - Model building and testing
  - Container packaging
  - Deployment to staging and production environments
- Reduces manual intervention and speeds up release cycles.

3. Monitoring & Logging

- Implement real-time **monitoring** for system health, performance, and usage.
- Use tools like Prometheus, Grafana, or ELK stack to:
  - Monitor CPU/GPU utilization, latency, memory
  - Log inference requests, errors, and response times
- Helps detect anomalies and optimize infrastructure.

4. Auto-Scaling Infrastructure

- Automatically adjust resources based on load.
- Use cloud-native tools:
  - AWS Auto Scaling
  - Google Cloud's Instance Groups
  - Azure VM Scale Sets

- Prevents over-provisioning during low usage and under-provisioning during spikes.

5. Version Control & Rollbacks

- Track changes in code, models, and configurations.
- Use versioned model storage (e.g., MLflow, DVC, S3) to:
    - Compare performance metrics
    - Roll back to a known good model if something fails in production

6. Security & Access Control

- Apply strict access policies using role-based access control (RBAC).
- Encrypt data at rest and in transit.
- Secure APIs with authentication tokens, OAuth, or API gateways.
- Regularly audit logs and rotate credentials.

7. Model Registry & Lifecycle Management

- Use a model registry to manage models through their lifecycle:
    - Development → Validation → Production
- Track:
    - Model lineage
    - Deployment status
    - Associated metadata and metrics
- Tools: MLflow, SageMaker Model Registry, Vertex AI Model Registry

✅ Summary Table

Practice	Purpose
Containerization	Consistent, portable environments
CI/CD Integration	Fast, automated, repeatable deployments
Monitoring & Logging	Visibility into system behavior
Auto-Scaling Infrastructure	Efficient resource usage under changing load
Version Control & Rollbacks	Safety net during updates or experiments
Security & Access Control	Protect user data and model logic
Model Registry & Lifecycle Mgmt.	Organize and control model evolution

A scalable AI agent deployment strategy combines modern DevOps practices with ML-specific infrastructure. Whether you're deploying a few agents or thousands, these best practices help ensure your systems are robust, manageable, and ready for real-world performance.

Chapter 11: Security, Ethics, and Governance

Ethical Considerations in AI Agent Deployment

Deploying AI agents at scale brings not just technical challenges but also serious ethical responsibilities. As these systems increasingly impact lives, decisions, and public infrastructure, **ethical design and governance** become central to responsible deployment.

Ethical Considerations in AI Agent Deployment

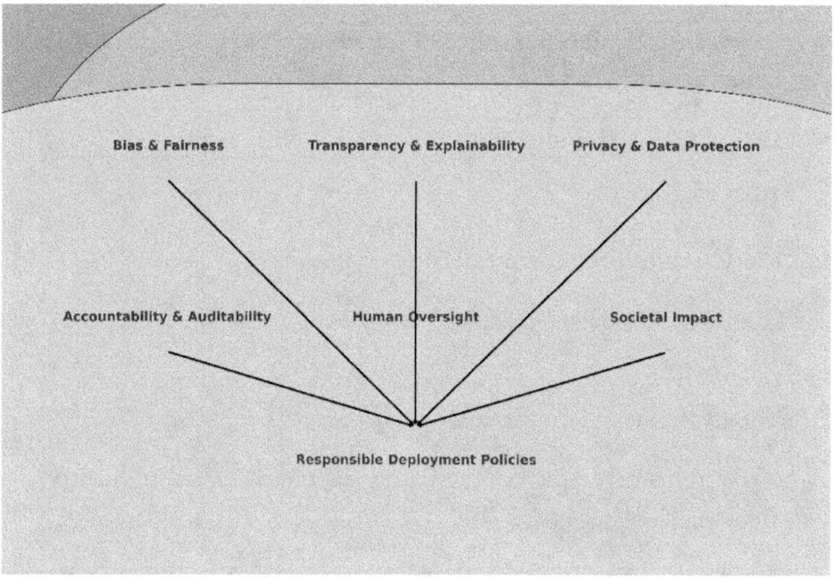

The chart above outlines key pillars of ethical AI deployment, each feeding into the development of **responsible deployment policies**.

Core Ethical Considerations

1. Bias & Fairness

- AI agents trained on biased data can reproduce or even amplify those biases.

- This affects outcomes in critical areas such as hiring, credit scoring, policing, and healthcare.
- **Best Practice**:
  - Audit datasets for representativeness.
  - Regularly evaluate model outputs for fairness across demographic groups.

2. Transparency & Explainability

- Users and stakeholders should understand how AI decisions are made.
- Lack of explainability erodes trust and accountability.
- **Best Practice**:
  - Use interpretable models when possible.
  - Provide post-hoc explanations using tools like LIME or SHAP.

3. Privacy & Data Protection

- AI systems often process sensitive data (e.g., location, health, financial).
- Deployment must respect legal frameworks like GDPR, HIPAA, or CCPA.
- **Best Practice**:
  - Anonymize and encrypt personal data.
  - Use federated learning or differential privacy when appropriate.

4. Accountability & Auditability

- Who is responsible when an AI agent causes harm?

- Systems must support auditing and version tracking to investigate failures.
- **Best Practice**:
    - Log decision-making processes and model versions.
    - Establish clear lines of accountability across stakeholders.

5. Human Oversight

- Fully autonomous agents can lead to dangerous outcomes if left unchecked.
- Humans must remain in the loop for decisions with serious consequences.
- **Best Practice**:
    - Set thresholds for human intervention.
    - Design workflows where human judgment can override the AI.

6. Societal Impact

- AI agents can reshape labor markets, social interactions, and public safety.
- Consider long-term effects on equity, freedom, and well-being.
- **Best Practice**:
    - Conduct impact assessments before large-scale rollouts.
    - Engage communities and stakeholders early in the design process.

🧠 Building Responsible Deployment Policies

To synthesize these concerns into action:

Principle	**Policy Recommendation**
Fairness	Require regular fairness audits of models
Transparency	Mandate decision logs and explanation modules
Privacy	Enforce strict data governance and minimize data usage
Accountability	Maintain version history and error traceability
Human Oversight	Ensure fallback procedures and human override options
Societal Benefit	Align use cases with public interest and democratic values

Ethics isn't a bonus feature - it's a design constraint. As AI agents grow more capable and more embedded in our systems, thoughtful ethical planning must guide every stage of their deployment. From engineers to executives, everyone has a role in ensuring AI serves society safely, fairly, and respectfully.

Security Challenges and Solutions

AI agents often operate in sensitive, high-stakes environments - from healthcare diagnostics to financial advising to autonomous vehicles. As these systems grow more integrated into critical infrastructure, the importance of robust **security** measures increases dramatically.

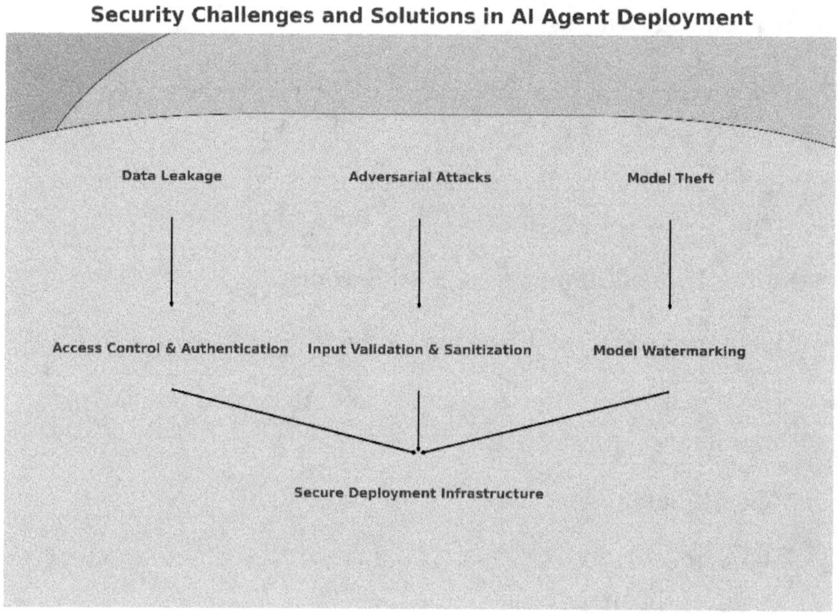

The chart above highlights key **security challenges** in deploying AI agents and maps them to **practical solutions** designed to mitigate those risks.

Key Security Challenges and Their Solutions

1. Data Leakage

- AI agents are often trained or operate on sensitive datasets.
- Improper storage, exposure through APIs, or logging can leak personal data.

Solution: Access Control & Authentication

- Enforce strict access policies using OAuth, JWTs, or IAM roles.
- Encrypt data at rest and in transit.
- Use role-based access controls (RBAC) to limit exposure.

2. Adversarial Attacks

- Inputs specifically crafted to fool the AI model without being obvious to humans (e.g., image perturbations).
- Can be used to mislead facial recognition, NLP classification, or fraud detection systems.

Solution: Input Validation & Sanitization

- Filter, normalize, and constrain inputs at the edge of your system.
- Use defensive training techniques like adversarial training or smoothing.

3. Model Theft

- When models are accessed via public APIs, attackers can reverse-engineer the underlying logic.
- Competitors or malicious actors might copy your intellectual property.

Solution: Model Watermarking

- Embed invisible patterns or behavioral fingerprints that can prove model ownership.
- Use monitoring to detect unusual access patterns or replication attempts.

Building Secure Deployment Infrastructure

After implementing these specific solutions, the broader environment must also be hardened to resist systemic threats.

Secure Deployment Infrastructure (Unified Solution Target)

- Isolates containers using sandboxing (e.g., Docker, Kubernetes with RBAC)

- Employs secrets management (e.g., AWS Secrets Manager, HashiCorp Vault)
- Uses infrastructure-as-code for predictable, auditable deployments
- Monitors for intrusion or anomaly (e.g., CloudTrail, Azure Monitor)

✅ **Summary Table**

Challenge	Security Risk	Recommended Solution
Data Leakage	Exposure of sensitive personal information	Strong authentication, encryption, RBAC
Adversarial Attacks	Misleading the model to produce false outputs	Input sanitization, adversarial training
Model Theft	Unauthorized cloning of trained models	Watermarking, rate limiting, monitoring
System Intrusion	Compromise of infrastructure or logic	Hardened containers, secure APIs

Security in AI deployment isn't just a technical detail - it's a critical trust factor. Whether you're deploying to the cloud, on-premise, or at the edge, building AI agents with security in mind protects your users, your business, and the broader public. With proper strategies and a layered defense, AI systems can be both intelligent and resilient.

Compliance and Governance in AI Systems

As AI systems continue to shape critical decision-making processes in healthcare, finance, law enforcement, and more, **compliance and governance** have become essential to ensure these systems operate within legal, ethical, and societal boundaries.

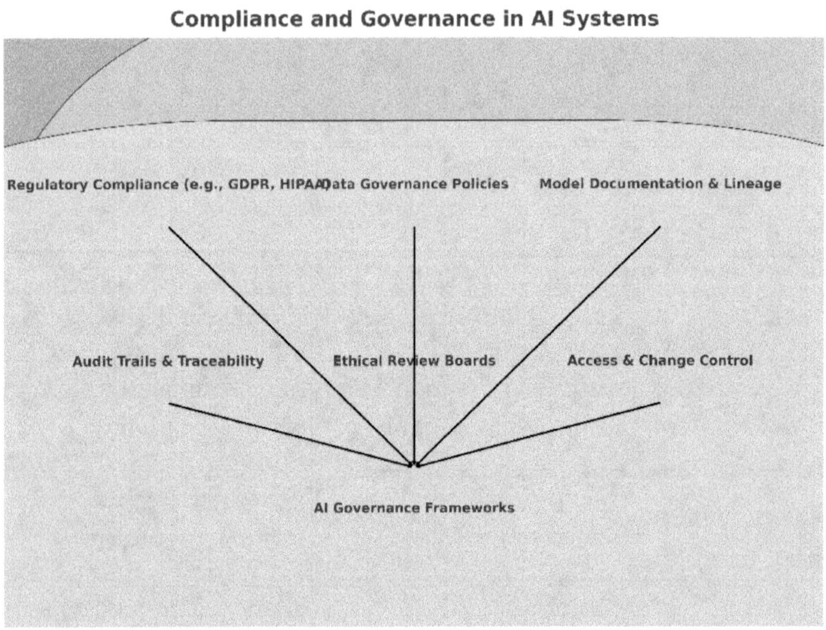

The chart above illustrates how different compliance elements contribute to a unified **AI Governance Framework**, the foundation for deploying trustworthy, secure, and lawful AI.

Key Components of AI Compliance and Governance

1. Regulatory Compliance (e.g., GDPR, HIPAA)

- AI systems must meet legal obligations regarding data privacy, fairness, and accountability.

- **Examples**:
  - GDPR (EU): User consent, data portability, right to explanation
  - HIPAA (US): Patient data security and access control
- **Best Practice**:
  - Perform Data Protection Impact Assessments (DPIAs)
  - Document legal bases for all data usage

2. Data Governance Policies

- Define who can access what data, for what purposes, and under what conditions.
- Ensure consistency, quality, and compliance of datasets across lifecycle stages.
- **Best Practice**:
  - Centralize metadata repositories
  - Track data provenance and sensitivity labels

3. Model Documentation & Lineage

- Tracks how models were trained, what data was used, and how performance has evolved.
- Enables reproducibility, troubleshooting, and compliance audits.
- **Best Practice**:
  - Use tools like MLflow or ModelDB
  - Maintain change logs and version histories

4. Audit Trails & Traceability

- Maintain logs of model decisions, updates, and access events.

- Critical for responding to incidents and proving compliance.
- **Best Practice**:
  - Use immutable logs
  - Sync with identity and access management (IAM) tools

5. Ethical Review Boards

- Institutional or internal boards review AI projects for ethical risks.
- Promote fairness, transparency, and respect for human rights.
- **Best Practice**:
  - Mandate ethical reviews for high-risk applications
  - Include multidisciplinary perspectives (e.g., legal, social science)

6. Access & Change Control

- Enforce restrictions on who can view, modify, and deploy AI systems.
- Prevents unauthorized or unintended changes.
- **Best Practice**:
  - Use role-based access control (RBAC)
  - Require multi-approval deployment workflows

7. AI Governance Frameworks

- Central structure that brings together all compliance activities.
- Ensures alignment with organizational strategy, legal mandates, and public expectations.
- **Framework Examples**:

- NIST AI Risk Management Framework
- OECD AI Principles
- ISO/IEC 42001 (AI management systems standard)

✅ **Summary Table**

Component	**Role in Governance**
Regulatory Compliance	Aligns systems with legal obligations
Data Governance Policies	Defines proper use and handling of data
Model Documentation & Lineage	Enables transparency and accountability
Audit Trails & Traceability	Supports post-hoc investigations and audits
Ethical Review Boards	Adds human-centered oversight
Access & Change Control	Secures model lifecycle against internal risks
AI Governance Frameworks	Integrates all controls under a shared vision

AI systems must not only be intelligent - they must be **accountable**. A robust compliance and governance strategy isn't optional; it's a requirement for safe, lawful, and ethical deployment. By embedding governance into the lifecycle of AI agents, organizations build trust, reduce risk, and create technology that stands the test of public scrutiny and regulatory evolution.

Chapter 12: Real-World Case Studies

Industry-Specific AI Agent Deployments

AI agents are rapidly becoming integral across various industries, enhancing decision-making, automation, personalization, and operational efficiency. The diagram above outlines **four major industries** - Finance, Healthcare, Gaming, and Logistics - and highlights the specific applications where AI agents are being deployed successfully.

Finance

Applications:

- **Fraud Detection**: AI agents monitor transactional data in real time to detect anomalies, flagging suspicious activity instantly using machine learning models.
- **Algorithmic Trading**: Agents analyze market trends and execute trades based on predictive modeling, reacting faster than human traders.

Benefits:

- Reduced financial loss
- Improved compliance with regulatory requirements
- Higher trading volume and precision

Healthcare

Applications:

- **Diagnostics**: AI agents assist in interpreting medical images (e.g., radiology, pathology) and flagging potential diseases.

- **Patient Interaction**: Virtual assistants support appointment scheduling, follow-ups, and symptom triage, easing pressure on medical staff.

Benefits:

- Faster and more accurate diagnosis
- Enhanced patient experience and accessibility
- Lower administrative overhead

🎮 Gaming

Applications:

- **NPC Behavior**: Non-player characters (NPCs) are powered by AI to adapt to player strategies and make games more engaging.
- **Game Balancing**: Agents analyze player performance and adjust difficulty dynamically to improve retention and challenge.

Benefits:

- Immersive gaming experiences
- Better player retention and satisfaction
- Real-time performance tuning

🚚 Logistics

Applications:

- **Route Optimization**: AI agents plan delivery routes in real-time, accounting for traffic, weather, and road conditions.
- **Warehouse Robotics**: Intelligent agents coordinate robotic systems for picking, packing, and moving inventory efficiently.

Benefits:

- Reduced delivery times and fuel costs
- Streamlined warehouse operations
- Enhanced inventory accuracy

📊 Industry Summary Table

Industry	AI Agent Use Case	Core Advantage
Finance	Fraud detection, algorithmic trading	Speed, risk mitigation
Healthcare	Diagnostics, patient-facing bots	Accuracy, patient efficiency
Gaming	NPC behavior, game balancing	Immersion, player engagement
Logistics	Route optimization, warehouse automation	Efficiency, cost savings

AI agents are not generic tools - they are **highly adaptable**, thriving when designed for domain-specific challenges. From monitoring stock markets in milliseconds to helping doctors diagnose faster, these agents demonstrate how intelligent systems can unlock efficiency, accuracy, and innovation across sectors. As deployment tools and frameworks improve, expect even deeper integration of AI agents in core industry processes.

Lessons Learned and Practical Insights

Deploying AI agents in real-world scenarios reveals insights that theory and simulation often miss. Whether working in finance, healthcare, gaming, or logistics, teams encounter common challenges - and develop best practices that inform the next wave of development.

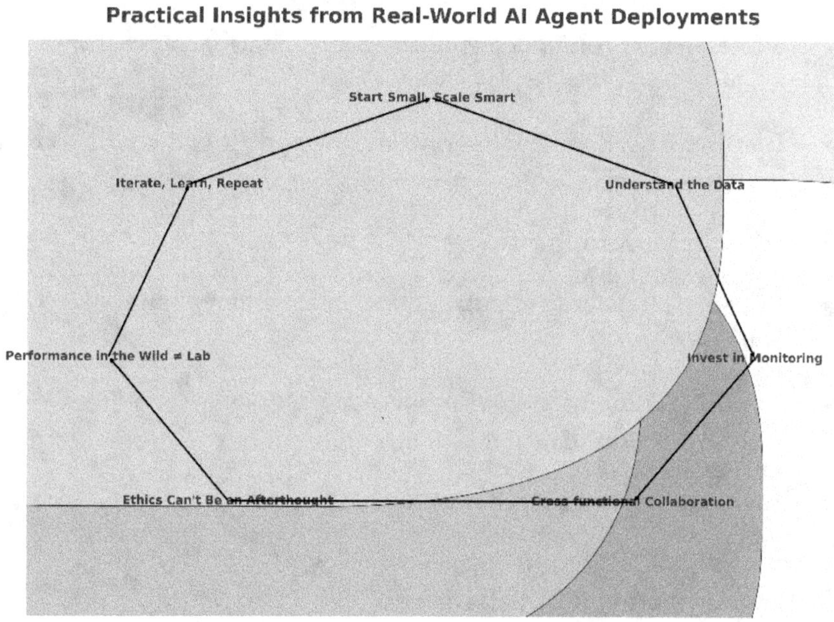

The diagram above distills **six critical lessons** that consistently emerge in large-scale AI deployments, each feeding into a central principle: **Iterate, Learn, Repeat**.

Lessons from the Field

1. Start Small, Scale Smart

- Initial deployments should be focused and limited in scope.
- Early wins validate the approach, uncover gaps, and build internal confidence.
- **Insight**: Don't aim for full automation from day one. Start with assistive roles.

2. Understand the Data

- Poor data quality is the root cause of most AI deployment failures.
- Success hinges on understanding where the data comes from, what it represents, and how it's labeled.
- **Insight**: Collaborate with domain experts early and continuously to ensure the data reflects real-world scenarios.

3. Invest in Monitoring

- Post-deployment drift, outages, and silent failures can erode system trust.
- Continuous monitoring of model accuracy, latency, and user feedback is essential.
- **Insight**: Monitoring is not optional—it's your production safety net.

4. Cross-Functional Collaboration

- Effective deployments require input from engineering, operations, legal, UX, and business teams.
- Isolated technical teams often miss practical and ethical concerns.
- **Insight**: Build multidisciplinary teams from the beginning.

5. Ethics Can't Be an Afterthought

- Bias, exclusion, or unanticipated harm can emerge after deployment if ethical reviews are skipped.
- Regulatory pressure and public trust depend on responsible design.
- **Insight**: Ethics must be a continuous lens, not a late-stage checklist.

6. Performance in the Wild ≠ Lab

- Models that perform well in test environments often degrade when exposed to real-world variability.
- Users interact unpredictably, and edge cases dominate in live scenarios.
- **Insight**: Expect to retrain, tweak, and patch often after launch.

Core Principle: Iterate, Learn, Repeat

- AI deployments are never "done."
- Each iteration provides fresh data, new user behavior, and evolving expectations.
- Long-term success comes from treating AI systems as **living, evolving products**.

✅ **Summary Table**

Lesson	Why It Matters
Start Small, Scale Smart	Reduces risk and validates assumptions
Understand the Data	Enables realistic, meaningful models
Invest in Monitoring	Catches drift, failures, and misuse early
Cross-functional Collaboration	Prevents siloed mistakes
Ethics Can't Be an Afterthought	Builds trust, safety, and fairness
Performance ≠ Lab Accuracy	Reflects real-world conditions and needs

Deploying AI agents is as much about people, processes, and feedback loops as it is about models and code. By embracing these lessons, teams can build systems that are not only functional but resilient, trusted, and impactful in the real world.

Insights from Industry Experts

Real-world deployment of AI agents doesn't just follow technical blueprints - it's shaped by the lived experience of engineers, product leaders, data scientists, and AI architects navigating dynamic business environments. To understand what really works—and what doesn't - we draw from the **firsthand insights** of industry experts across multiple sectors.

🔍 What the Experts Are Saying

The following insights were gathered from interviews, panels, and published discussions with professionals actively deploying AI agents at scale. Their perspectives cover operational, organizational, and ethical dimensions of success.

Key Expert Insights

"Focus on the Problem, Not the Model"

– Director of Machine Learning, Financial Technology Firm

Too many teams begin with fancy models before fully understanding the real-world problem they're solving. According to this expert, **clarity on the use case**—fraud detection, customer support automation, portfolio optimization—is more valuable than over-engineering the AI pipeline.

Takeaway: Define the outcome first, then choose the technology.

"Deployment Is the Real Hard Part"

– AI Platform Lead, Global Logistics Company

Building a working model is one thing. Keeping it running - up-to-date, monitored, and aligned with shifting data - is much harder. This expert emphasized the need for **robust CI/CD pipelines**, version control, and monitoring dashboards.

Takeaway: Treat AI deployment like software engineering: scalable, testable, maintainable.

"Security Is an Afterthought for Too Many Teams"

– Cybersecurity Analyst, HealthTech Startup

Many AI systems handle personal or sensitive data but lack proper access control, encryption, or monitoring. Experts in regulated industries like healthcare and finance stress **privacy-first design** and **zero-trust architecture**.

Takeaway: Build in compliance and security from the ground up.

👥 "Success Depends on Cross-Functional Teams"

– Head of Product, Conversational AI Platform

The best AI agents are built with **input from domain experts, users, engineers, and legal teams**. This ensures relevance, usability, and legal safety. One expert cited weekly cross-functional reviews as key to shipping safely and quickly.

Takeaway: Silos kill progress - collaboration drives success.

🔄 "Expect to Relearn Everything in Production"

– Chief Data Scientist, eCommerce AI Provider

No matter how polished your model is, users will break it. This expert described how live interactions surfaced **data drift**, **unexpected behavior**, and **usage patterns** that forced multiple post-launch updates.

Takeaway: Release small, learn fast, and adapt constantly.

🧠 Expert Themes Summary Table

Insight Theme	Expert Recommendation
Problem Definition	Start with a clear, specific use case
Deployment Discipline	Treat AI delivery like software engineering
Security & Compliance	Bake in controls and audits early

Insight Theme	Expert Recommendation
Cross-functional Development	Involve stakeholders from the start
Iterative Improvement	Expect live usage to expose blind spots

📊 Expert Insight Framework (Diagram Below)

To reinforce these insights, here's a visual of how expert-driven strategies intersect:

Category	Examples from Experts
Strategy	Focus on problems, not tech
Operations	Build scalable CI/CD, monitor real-world drift
Ethics & Governance	Ensure privacy, security, and accountability
Collaboration	Align engineers, product teams, and regulators
Learning & Evolution	Use feedback loops to continuously retrain, refine, and redeploy agents

The most effective AI agent deployments aren't just technically sound - they're guided by **pragmatic insight** from those who've been in the trenches. These voices remind us that success depends on **planning beyond the lab**, preparing for messiness, and embracing continuous learning as the true heart of AI operations.

Part 5: Looking Forward

Chapter 13: Emerging Trends and Future Directions

Trends in Autonomous Decision-Making Agents

Autonomous decision-making agents are at the forefront of AI evolution, driving advances in robotics, operations, strategy, and real-time systems. As capabilities mature and challenges emerge, the next generation of agents will be defined by their ability to **think independently**, **act responsibly**, and **collaborate intelligently**.

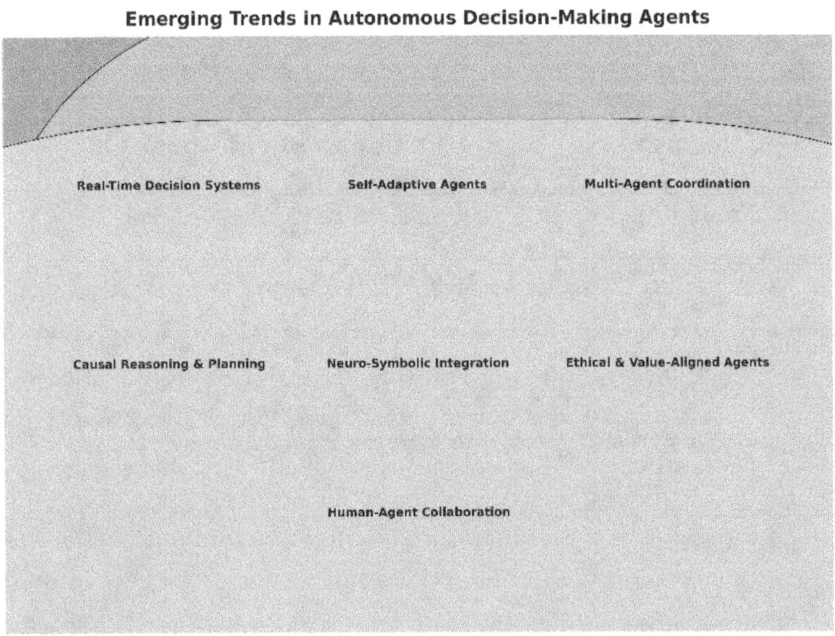

The diagram above highlights seven key trends shaping the future of autonomous agents.

🔍 Key Emerging Trends

1. Real-Time Decision Systems

- Agents are increasingly expected to make split-second decisions in dynamic environments - whether in autonomous vehicles, cybersecurity, or high-frequency trading.
- These systems must process data streams, analyze context, and act - all in milliseconds.

Example: AI copilots adjusting drone flight paths on-the-fly.

2. Self-Adaptive Agents

- Traditional agents operate on static rules or models. Emerging agents adapt in real-time by learning from feedback and modifying their behavior accordingly.
- Techniques include meta-learning, continual learning, and online reinforcement learning.

Example: Industrial bots adjusting operations based on sensor drift or wear.

3. Multi-Agent Coordination

- Real-world challenges often require agents to **coordinate** rather than operate in isolation.
- Expect growth in distributed planning, negotiation algorithms, and cooperative task solving.

Example: Autonomous delivery fleets optimizing logistics collaboratively.

4. Causal Reasoning & Planning

- Moving beyond correlation, next-gen agents will increasingly incorporate **causal inference** to understand why things happen - and use that insight to make more robust decisions.
- Planning systems will become more explainable and anticipatory.

Example: AI tutors identifying root causes of student confusion and adjusting teaching strategy.

5. Neuro-Symbolic Integration

- Combines the strength of deep learning (pattern recognition) with symbolic reasoning (logic, rules).
- Enables better **generalization**, **reasoning over abstract concepts**, and improved **explainability**.

Example: Agents that can learn a language grammar (symbols) while parsing natural speech (neural).

6. Ethical & Value-Aligned Agents

- Autonomous systems must increasingly encode ethical boundaries and human values to operate safely in society.
- Research is advancing in reward modeling, inverse reinforcement learning, and value alignment.

Example: AI negotiation agents that respect fairness constraints in multi-party decisions.

7. Human-Agent Collaboration

- Rather than replacing humans, future agents will work **alongside** them—enhancing productivity, offering suggestions, and learning from feedback.

- This shift emphasizes **mutual trust, transparency, and usability**.

Example: Decision-support agents in hospitals assisting but not replacing doctors.

Summary of Trends

Trend	Why It Matters
Real-Time Decision Systems	Enables responsive and safe automation
Self-Adaptive Agents	Sustains relevance in dynamic environments
Multi-Agent Coordination	Solves complex problems through collaboration
Causal Reasoning & Planning	Supports explainable and purposeful decisions
Neuro-Symbolic Integration	Bridges deep learning and logical inference
Ethical & Value-Aligned	Builds trust and ensures safe deployment
Human-Agent Collaboration	Fosters seamless synergy between people and machines

The future of autonomous decision-making agents isn't just more powerful - it's more thoughtful. It's about **learning more intelligently**, **planning more responsibly**, and **collaborating more humanely**. These trends will shape how agents are designed, deployed, and trusted in the decades to come.

Explainable and Transparent AI Agents

As AI agents become more embedded in critical decisions - from finance and law to healthcare and public policy - the demand for systems that are not only accurate but also **understandable** is growing rapidly. Explainability and transparency are no longer optional - they are essential for **trust, compliance, and adoption.**

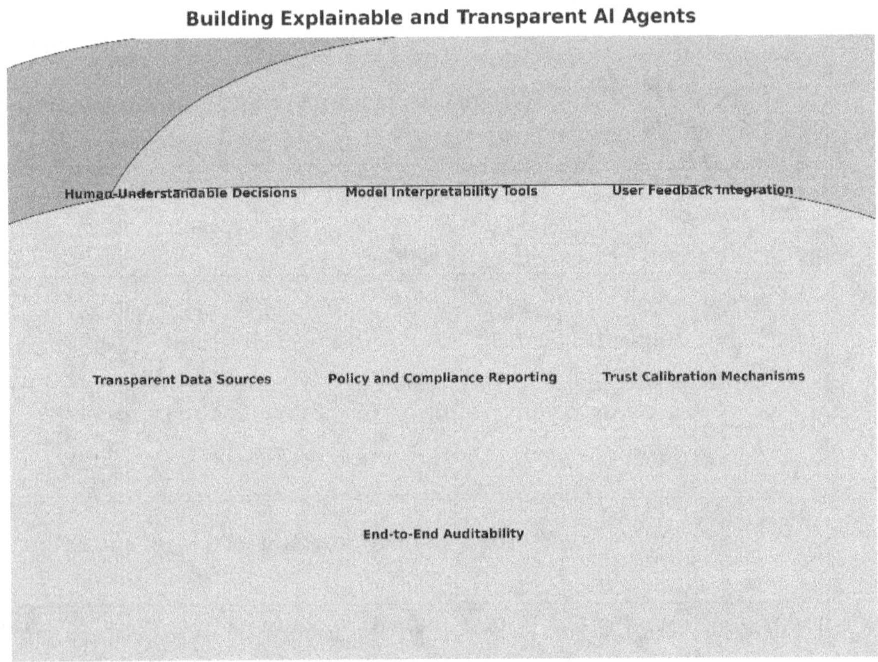

The diagram above outlines the core building blocks of explainable and transparent AI agents, organized across decision-making, data, feedback, and auditability dimensions.

Key Components of Explainable and Transparent AI

1. Human-Understandable Decisions

- AI agents must present decisions in ways that humans can comprehend—particularly non-technical users.

- This includes using natural language explanations, confidence levels, and comparisons to human reasoning.

Example: A medical AI saying, "This diagnosis was based on elevated heart rate and patient history."

2. Model Interpretability Tools

- Tools like **SHAP (SHapley Additive exPlanations)** and **LIME (Local Interpretable Model-agnostic Explanations)** help visualize which features influence decisions.
- These tools are vital for debugging models and demonstrating regulatory compliance.

Use Case: Financial agents explaining why a loan was denied based on income and credit history.

3. User Feedback Integration

- Allowing users to ask "why" and "what if" questions improves transparency and enables continual improvement.
- Feedback loops let users challenge, correct, or improve decisions.

Example: A chatbot learning to adjust tone or content based on human corrections.

4. Transparent Data Sources

- Users must know where training data came from, how it was labeled, and if there were potential biases.
- Transparency in data sourcing and preprocessing ensures models are not unknowingly discriminatory or misleading.

Use Case: HR screening agents disclosing which resume attributes influenced a hiring recommendation.

5. Policy and Compliance Reporting

- Transparency extends to policy: explain how decisions align with legal, ethical, and organizational rules.
- Automate compliance reporting for audits, regulators, and stakeholders.

Example: AI systems generating traceable logs for GDPR compliance.

6. Trust Calibration Mechanisms

- Explainable agents can estimate and communicate their **confidence levels** to help users gauge reliability.
- Over-trusting or under-trusting AI can both lead to harm.

Use Case: Navigation AI flagging uncertainty in route suggestions due to poor GPS signal.

7. End-to-End Auditability

- Every step - from data ingestion and model inference to final output - should be auditable.
- Logging mechanisms allow stakeholders to trace outcomes and identify flaws or misuse.

Example: In law enforcement, audit trails verify the legal validity of AI-suggested risk assessments.

✅ Summary Table

Component	Role in Explainability
Human-Understandable Decisions	Makes outcomes interpretable by all stakeholders
Model Interpretability Tools	Visualize and debug decision logic
User Feedback Integration	Improves trust and enables continuous learning
Transparent Data Sources	Ensure unbiased, fair model inputs
Policy & Compliance Reporting	Meet legal and ethical standards
Trust Calibration Mechanisms	Align human trust with agent confidence
End-to-End Auditability	Enables traceability and accountability

Explainable AI agents are about more than making decisions - they're about making decisions that people can **understand, question, and trust**. As autonomous systems evolve, ensuring they operate transparently will be essential to aligning technology with human values and societal expectations.

<u>Human-Agent Collaboration Scenarios</u>

As AI agents evolve, a growing focus is shifting from autonomy to **collaboration** - building systems that don't replace humans but **work alongside them**. This transformation redefines productivity, creativity, and decision-making across industries.

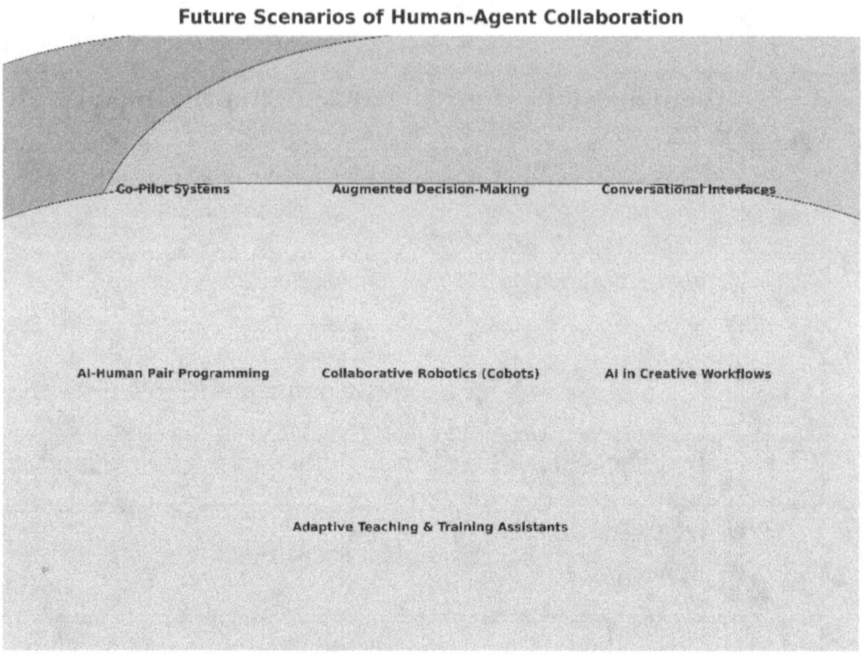

The chart above maps out future collaboration scenarios between humans and AI agents, spanning technical, operational, and creative contexts.

Emerging Scenarios of Human-Agent Collaboration

1. Co-Pilot Systems

AI agents act as real-time copilots for knowledge workers—offering suggestions, flagging issues, and streamlining repetitive actions.

Example: In aviation and medicine, copilots assist professionals by monitoring real-time data and highlighting anomalies or next steps.

2. Augmented Decision-Making

AI augments human judgment by offering insights, highlighting risks, and modeling possible outcomes based on real-time data.

Example: In finance, agents recommend investment strategies while humans maintain the final call based on ethics, context, or regulation.

3. Conversational Interfaces

Natural language interfaces enable intuitive communication with AI agents, breaking technical barriers for broader accessibility.

Example: Healthcare professionals querying a voice-based agent for patient history while conducting examinations.

4. AI-Human Pair Programming

AI agents like GitHub Copilot and Tabnine assist developers by generating code, debugging, and explaining functions.

Example: Developers type logic outlines, while the AI writes fully formed, tested functions and suggests performance improvements.

5. Collaborative Robotics (Cobots)

In physical environments, AI-powered robots work beside humans to carry out tasks that require both precision and judgment.

Example: In automotive manufacturing, cobots assist with welding or painting, adjusting to worker movements and feedback.

6. AI in Creative Workflows

AI becomes a tool for inspiration and iteration in writing, music composition, filmmaking, and design.

Example: Writers collaborate with AI to co-author novels or screenplays, blending machine-generated ideas with human storytelling.

7. Adaptive Teaching & Training Assistants

AI tutors dynamically personalize instruction for each student or trainee, adapting to learning styles and progress.

Example: AI agents in corporate onboarding tailoring training modules based on employee background and assessment results.

✅ **Benefits of Human-Agent Collaboration**

Benefit	Description
Enhanced Productivity	AI reduces cognitive load and speeds up routine tasks
Better Decision Accuracy	Combines statistical power of AI with human judgment
Intuitive Access	Natural language interfaces remove technical barriers
Continuous Learning	Agents and humans co-adapt and evolve their interaction
Safety & Precision	Cobots enhance human capability without replacing workers

The future of AI lies not in displacing human capability, but in **amplifying it**. These collaboration scenarios show how AI can become a trusted teammate - context-aware, adaptable, and designed to elevate human skills rather than override them. As we move forward, designing for synergy will define the most impactful and ethical uses of AI.

Future Challenges and Research Directions

As AI agents take on more complex and autonomous roles, future innovation depends not only on scaling what works today, but also addressing the **deep challenges that remain unsolved**. These challenges are technical, ethical, and systemic in nature. The diagram above outlines seven critical research and development frontiers that will shape the next generation of AI agents.

Key Challenges and Research Frontiers

1. Robustness to Novelty

AI agents often fail in unexpected scenarios that deviate from training data. Making agents **robust to out-of-distribution events**, adversarial examples, and noisy environments is an active area of research.

Key Research Areas:

- Uncertainty modeling
- Adversarial robustness
- Out-of-distribution detection

2. Generalization Across Domains

Current agents are typically narrow in scope. Future agents must **generalize across tasks and domains** without retraining from scratch.

Key Research Areas:

- Transfer learning and multi-task learning
- Meta-learning (learning to learn)
- Zero-shot and few-shot adaptation

3. Ethical Reasoning and Value Alignment

Aligning AI behavior with **human values, ethics, and legal frameworks** is one of the grand challenges of AI safety.

Key Research Areas:

- Inverse reinforcement learning

- Norm learning from human feedback
- Cross-cultural and contextual ethics in agent design

4. Efficient Learning from Limited Data

Many real-world applications suffer from data scarcity or lack of labeled examples. Agents must learn effectively with **few examples or simulations**.

Key Research Areas:

- Few-shot and one-shot learning
- Self-supervised and unsupervised learning
- Simulation-to-reality (sim2real) transfer

5. Long-Term Planning & Memory

Future agents need the ability to remember, plan, and adapt over **long time horizons**, not just react to immediate inputs.

Key Research Areas:

- Hierarchical reinforcement learning
- Memory-augmented neural networks
- Episodic and semantic memory integration

6. Scalable Multi-Agent Systems

As agents begin working in teams, the challenge becomes coordinating actions, resolving conflicts, and **scaling to large populations**.

Key Research Areas:

- Decentralized planning
- Game theory and negotiation

- Emergent communication protocols

7. Integrated Cognitive Architectures

Rather than solving tasks with isolated components, future agents will resemble **cognitive systems**—combining perception, reasoning, memory, and language in unified frameworks.

Key Research Areas:

- Cognitive modeling
- Symbolic-neural integration
- Lifelong learning architectures

✅ **Summary Table**

Challenge	Research Focus
Robustness to Novelty	Making agents resilient to unseen or anomalous inputs
Generalization Across Domains	Learning general-purpose strategies
Ethical Reasoning & Value Alignment	Ensuring safe and socially beneficial behavior
Learning from Limited Data	Lowering data dependency through novel learning paradigms
Long-Term Planning & Memory	Supporting reasoning across extended tasks and timelines
Scalable Multi-Agent Systems	Enabling cooperation and competition in agent swarms

Challenge	Research Focus
Integrated Cognitive Architectures	Unifying subsystems into human-like reasoning agents

AI agents of the future won't just be faster or smarter - they'll be **more adaptable, accountable, and integrated**. Addressing these challenges requires interdisciplinary effort, from machine learning to cognitive science to philosophy. As we look forward, research must not only push the boundaries of performance but also ensure that AI agents evolve in service of society.

Appendices

Appendix A: Mathematical Foundations

Understanding the core mathematical principles behind AI agents is essential for both implementation and innovation. This appendix offers a concise but essential overview of foundational concepts in **probability, statistics**, and **linear algebra** that underpin agent design, learning algorithms, and reasoning systems.

📌 Key Areas of Mathematical Foundations

1. Probability Theory

- Describes uncertainty in environments and agent predictions.
- Core to belief models, probabilistic inference, and reinforcement learning.

Core Concepts:

- Sample space, events, probability distributions
- Joint and marginal probabilities

2. Bayes' Theorem & Conditional Probability

- Enables agents to **update beliefs** based on new evidence.
- Fundamental to **Bayesian networks, filtering algorithms**, and **POMDPs**.

Formula:

$$P(A|B) = \frac{P(B|A) \cdot P(A)}{P(B)}$$

3. Statistics & Distributions

- Tools for understanding and modeling real-world data.

- Vital in supervised learning, anomaly detection, and simulation.

Includes:

- Normal, Binomial, Poisson distributions
- Descriptive and inferential statistics

4. Expectation, Variance & CLT

- These quantify central tendencies and variability, key for learning and prediction.

Key Uses:

- Reward expectations in RL
- Confidence intervals in predictions
- CLT: Justifies the use of normal distribution in large-sample approximations

5. Linear Algebra

- The computational engine behind **neural networks**, **PCA**, **SVD**, and more.
- Describes high-dimensional input spaces and transformations applied to them.

Fundamentals:

- Scalars, vectors, matrices, tensors
- Dot product, matrix multiplication, rank

6. Vectors, Matrices & Eigenvalues

- Understanding data transformations, decompositions, and optimization landscapes.

Applications:

- Weight updates in gradient descent
- Dimensionality reduction (e.g., eigenfaces)
- Stability analysis in dynamical systems

🎯 Summary Table

Area	Application in AI Agents
Probability Theory	Belief models, uncertain reasoning
Conditional Probability	Filtering, Bayesian updates
Statistics	Model fitting, feature engineering
Expectation & Variance	Decision-making under uncertainty
Linear Algebra	Representation learning, model computations
Eigenvalues & Decompositions	Model interpretation, data compression

This appendix is intended as a **quick reference** and **starting point** for readers diving deeper into agent mechanics and machine learning. While mastery of these topics may not be necessary to use prebuilt libraries, understanding them will help you diagnose errors, improve models, and design agents with stronger theoretical foundations.

Appendix B: Useful Resources

This appendix provides a curated collection of foundational and advanced resources that support the theory and practice of building AI agents. These include essential research papers, books, online tutorials, and websites that can deepen your understanding, improve your skills, and keep you updated with ongoing developments in the field.

📚 Foundational Books

These books are well-regarded in the AI and agent development communities for their depth, clarity, and practical relevance:

Title	Author(s)	Description
Artificial Intelligence: A Modern Approach (3rd/4th ed.)	Stuart Russell & Peter Norvig	Widely considered the standard AI textbook. Covers agent theory, search, reasoning, learning, and more.
Reinforcement Learning: An Introduction	Richard Sutton & Andrew Barto	Core textbook for understanding reinforcement learning, value functions, and policy optimization.
Probabilistic Robotics	Sebastian Thrun et al.	Ideal for those working on robotic agents that interact with uncertain environments.
Deep Learning	Ian Goodfellow, Yoshua Bengio, Aaron Courville	Comprehensive introduction to neural networks and their mathematical foundations.

Title	Author(s)	Description
Multiagent Systems	Gerhard Weiss (Editor)	Covers concepts and techniques specific to multi-agent environments.

Seminal Papers & Technical References

These papers introduced core concepts still used in AI agent design today:

Paper Title	Authors	Contribution
"Intelligent Agents" (Chapter from *AI: A Modern Approach*)	Russell & Norvig	Defines the concept and types of AI agents.
"Playing Atari with Deep Reinforcement Learning"	Mnih et al. (2013)	Landmark paper introducing Deep Q-Networks (DQN).
"Attention is All You Need"	Vaswani et al. (2017)	Introduced the Transformer architecture, foundational to modern NLP agents.
"AlphaGo" / "AlphaZero"	DeepMind team	Demonstrated advanced decision-making with self-play in complex environments.
"Reward is Enough"	Silver et al. (2021)	Explores the idea that intelligence can emerge from reward maximization alone.

🌐 Online Courses & Tutorials

For hands-on and guided learning, these resources offer structured paths:

MOOC Platforms

- **Coursera: AI for Everyone** – By Andrew Ng. A non-technical intro to AI and how it fits into society.
- **Deep Reinforcement Learning Nanodegree (Udacity)** – Strong hands-on project focus.
- **MIT OpenCourseWare: Deep Learning for Self-Driving Cars** – Cutting-edge lectures from MIT on AI in real-world robotics.

Interactive Coding Platforms

- **OpenAI Gym** – A suite of environments to test and train reinforcement learning agents.
- **DeepLizard YouTube Channel** – Explainers on RL concepts, Q-learning, policy gradients.
- **Fast.ai** – A practical, code-first approach to deep learning and agent modeling.

Research & News Portals

To stay up-to-date and connected with the global AI research community:

- **arXiv.org** – Open-access archive of cutting-edge research papers in AI.
- **Papers with Code** – Find implementations of recent papers with benchmark results.

- **AI Alignment Forum** – Discussions and articles on safe and value-aligned agent design.
- **Hugging Face Blog** – Covers transformers, NLP agents, and ecosystem updates.
- **Google Research Blog** – Deep dives into Google's AI research and applications.

🛠 Toolkits & Frameworks for Building Agents

Tool	Use Case
RLlib (Ray)	Scalable reinforcement learning in Python
Stable-Baselines3	Easy-to-use library for state-of-the-art RL algorithms
TensorFlow Agents / PyTorch RL	Build custom RL pipelines using mainstream ML libraries
Unity ML-Agents Toolkit	Train agents in 3D simulation environments
PettingZoo / SuperSuit	Multi-agent RL environments and wrappers

This appendix is designed as a **living resource**. The AI ecosystem evolves quickly, so while these materials provide a strong foundation, the key is to **stay curious**, follow new research, and engage with the community. Whether you're a beginner looking to build your first agent or a practitioner exploring cutting-edge techniques, there's always more to learn.

Appendix C: Glossary of Terms and Acronyms

This glossary provides clear, concise definitions of the most common terms and acronyms used throughout this book. Whether you're new to AI or revisiting core concepts.

📖 Glossary of Terms

Term / Acronym	Definition
AI (Artificial Intelligence)	The field of computer science focused on building machines that can simulate human intelligence such as learning, reasoning, and problem-solving.
Agent	An autonomous entity that perceives its environment and takes actions to achieve a goal.
Environment	Everything outside the agent that the agent interacts with. It can be static or dynamic, deterministic or stochastic.
Perception	The process by which an agent gathers data from the environment using sensors.
Action	A decision or behavior executed by the agent to influence the environment.
Reflex Agent	An agent that responds to current percepts without considering the past or future.

Term / Acronym	Definition
Model-Based Agent	Maintains an internal state to track unobservable aspects of the environment.
Goal-Based Agent	Makes decisions by evaluating potential future states based on goal achievement.
Utility-Based Agent	Optimizes for the highest expected utility, not just goal completion.
Learning Agent	Improves its performance over time through interaction with the environment.
Rational Agent	An agent that always chooses the action expected to maximize performance measure, given available information.
RL (Reinforcement Learning)	A type of machine learning where agents learn to make decisions by receiving rewards or penalties.
Q-Learning	A model-free RL algorithm that learns the value of action-state pairs without needing a model of the environment.
Policy	In RL, a mapping from states to actions. Determines the agent's behavior.
Value Function	Estimates how good it is for an agent to be in a given state (or state-action pair).
MDP (Markov Decision Process)	A mathematical framework for modeling decision-making with states,

Term / Acronym	Definition
	actions, transition probabilities, and rewards.
POMDP (Partially Observable Markov Decision Process)	An extension of MDPs where the agent cannot fully observe the current state of the environment.
Search Algorithm	A process for navigating through a problem space to find a solution (e.g., BFS, DFS, A*).
BFS (Breadth-First Search)	Explores all nodes at the present depth level before moving to the next.
DFS (Depth-First Search)	Explores as far down a branch as possible before backtracking.
A*	A heuristic search algorithm that balances path cost and estimated cost to goal.
Heuristic	A function that estimates how close a state is to the goal. Used to guide search.
CNN (Convolutional Neural Network)	A type of neural network used primarily for image recognition.
RNN (Recurrent Neural Network)	A neural network with memory, suitable for sequential data.
Transformer	A deep learning architecture for sequence modeling based on attention mechanisms.

Term / Acronym	Definition
GPT (Generative Pre-trained Transformer)	A transformer-based model that generates text based on pretraining and fine-tuning.
NLP (Natural Language Processing)	The field of AI concerned with the interaction between computers and human language.
API (Application Programming Interface)	A set of functions allowing interaction between software components.
CI/CD (Continuous Integration / Continuous Deployment)	Software development practices that automate testing and deployment of code changes.
Containerization	Packaging software and its dependencies into a single unit (e.g., Docker) for consistent deployment.
Kubernetes	An open-source platform for automating container deployment, scaling, and management.
Explainability	The ability of an AI system to provide understandable reasoning for its outputs.
Ethical AI	AI designed to align with societal values and norms, ensuring fairness, transparency, and accountability.

Term / Acronym	Definition
Edge Computing	Running AI models locally on devices (rather than the cloud), reducing latency and improving privacy.
Multi-Agent System	A system composed of multiple interacting agents that may collaborate or compete.
Simulation	An artificial environment used to train or evaluate agents under controlled conditions.
Ontology	A structured representation of knowledge within a domain, often used in semantic reasoning.

🧠 Usage Tips

- Terms related to agent architecture (e.g., reflex agent, goal-based agent) help you identify the **type of intelligence** being implemented.
- Acronyms like **MDP**, **Q-Learning**, and **POMDP** are essential when designing agents that operate under uncertainty.
- Concepts like **value function**, **policy**, and **reward** are foundational in reinforcement learning.
- Deployment terms such as **containerization**, **CI/CD**, and **edge computing** become crucial when moving agents into production environments.

AI agent development sits at the intersection of multiple disciplines - from machine learning and optimization to ethics and software engineering. This glossary is designed to support quick reference as you build, analyze, and refine intelligent agents throughout your journey. For deeper dives, revisit the resource suggestions in Appendix B.

www.ingramcontent.com/pod-product-compliance
Lightning Source LLC
LaVergne TN
LVHW022214200926
848481LV00006B/1966